Dr Peter Collins is Senior Lecturer in History at St Mary's University College, Belfast. He is Secretary of the United Irishmen Commemoration Society (UICS) in Belfast.

Who *fears* to Speak *of* '98?

Commemoration and the continuing
impact of the United Irishmen

PETER COLLINS

ULSTER HISTORICAL
FOUNDATION

This work is dedicated to
my wife Noreen and our children Patrick,
Catherine, Andrew and Sean.

It was proposed to me that I should help to uplift my downtrodden country by assembling with other Irishmen to romance about 1798. I do not take the slightest interest in 1798. Until Irishmen apply themselves seriously to what the condition of Ireland is to be in 1998 they will get very little patriotism out of yours sincerely GBS.

George Bernard Shaw, 1898

1798.

NIL DESPERANDUM.

This book has received support from the Northern Ireland Community Relations Council which promotes a pluralist society characterised by equity, respect for diversity and interdependence. The views expressed do not necessarily reflect those of the Community Relations Council.

The Ulster Historical Foundation is also pleased to acknowledge support for this publication provided by the Department of the Taoiseach, Dublin.

First published 2004
by the Ulster Historical Foundation
12 College Square East, Belfast BT1 6DD
www.ancestryireland.com

© Peter Collins
ISBN 1-903688-23-X

Printed by ColourBooks Ltd, Dublin
Design by Dunbar Design

Contents

Acknowledgements

I first wish to thank the Cultural Diversities Committee of the Northern Ireland Community Relations Council (CRC) for awarding me a Fellowship to undertake this work. I am grateful to Maurna Crozier and Malcolm Scott of that body for their support and advice. I would also like to record my thanks to the Northern Ireland Community Relations Council, for financial support given to enable publication of this research. The Department of An Taoiseach, Bertie Ahern, through the good offices of Dr Martin Mansergh, also provided generous funding toward the production of this book and I am very grateful to them.

The members of the United Irishmen Commemoration Society (UICS) provided enthusiastic support and advice throughout, especially during our extremely enjoyable peregrinations to the sites of '98. In particular I am grateful to John Gray, Chair of UICS, for his friendship, knowledge and advice generously shared and his infectious enthusiasm for the project. By the same token, I wish to thank his predecessor Eamon Hanna for his support. I am especially grateful to UICS stalwart Art McMillen who selflessly provided a constant flood of very useful material. UICS executive members, Raymond Shearer and John Neill, both helped greatly with illustrative material and suggestions.

Without visits to the sites of '98 the picture would have been incomplete. I am very grateful to all those who provided support and guidance to myself and the UICS on tour. In this respect UICS member Bill Wilsdon took us on three visits to the sites of Counties Antrim and Down, the subject of his excellent book. Bernard Browne, Brian Clery, and Nicky Furlong were our hosts and guides in Co.Wexford. Bernard was also extremely generous in supplying me from his own resources much essential material. Rúan O'Donnell was a very cogent guide on the UICS tour of the sites of Co.Wicklow, on which he is undoubtedly the leading authority. Alice Kearney, the driving force in the Republic's 1798 Commemoration body, headed by Minister Seamus Brennan, TD provided me with many invitations to official commemorative events in 1998 which enabled me to compile the section on the bicentenary in the south.

Many members of local councils, other public bodies and local history societies greatly helped the project by organising commemorative events and producing related publications. These include Keith Beattie, Damien Brannigan, Jane Leonard, and Gary Shaw.

In Tom Bartlett, David Dickson, Tommy Graham, Daire Keogh, Rúan O'Donnell and Kevin Whelan, I am very lucky to have as colleagues and friends the people who collectively have produced a groundbreaking corpus of recent history of 1798. Amazingly they found the time to roll up their sleeves and organise many commemorative events, in between rushing around the country fulfilling engagements as the most sought after speakers. No wonder they became known as 'The Usual Suspects'. Kevin and Tom in particular provided me with much valuable material and advice. Virginia Crossman, Catherine Morris and Rev Finlay Holmes selflessly allowed me access to and permission to quote from their writings both published and unpublished. I wish to thank Larry McBride for his advice and help.

A special thanks is due to the following who responded generously to my request for perspectives on the commemorative events of 1998. In so doing they provided a very fitting epilogue to the bicentenary year. They are Damien Brannigan, Bernard Browne, David Hall, Brian Kennaway, Daire Keogh, A.T.Q. Stewart, and Kevin Whelan. UICS member, James Stewart, generously allowed me to include an extract from his as yet unpublished work on 1948.

My particular thanks go to the Ulster Historical Foundation for publishing this work. I am very grateful to Fintan Mullan and his staff for their assistance. Wendy Dunbar has done a great job in its design and layout. Thanks are also due to Brendan O'Brien for copyediting the work and suggesting improvements, and to Helen Litton for compiling the index.

Finally, if I have inadvertently omitted some who have helped me, please nevertheless accept my thanks. Neither they nor any others mentioned above are responsible for errors contained in this work.

Preface

This work originated in a Cultural Traditions Fellowship awarded in 1998 by the Cultural Diversities Committee of the Northern Ireland Community Relations Council. For the Fellowship, the Committee asked me to write an account of historical commemoration of '98. This area, of course, has already received considerable attention from historians. I was asked to give particular consideration to recent commemoration of '98, especially the bicentenary in 1998. A major part of my treatment of the bicentenary was to take the form of a calendar of events. In addition, as part of my Fellowship, I was to act as organiser during the bicentenary for the United Irishmen Commemoration Society based in the Linen Hall Library and chaired originally by Eamon Hanna and latterly by John Gray.

1998, as well as being the bicentenary of the Rising of the United Irishmen, was a year of great hope and equally great despair in the political process. The signing in April of the Good Friday Agreement received massive acceptance in referenda north and south. The Agreement promised equality and a say in their own destiny to all the people in the north for the first time. As such, it could be said to reflect the aims of the United Irishmen. The Omagh bombing in August 1998 was one of the darkest days in Irish history, and threatened at the outset the bright promise of only a few months earlier. As such, it was reminiscent of the disaster that afflicted Ireland in the Rising of the summer of 1798.

In every generation since 1798 there has been commemoration of the United Irishmen. In many respects, the manner in which this has been observed has been an indicator of the state of politics in the Ireland of the day. An important corollary has been the nature and level of opposition to commemoration of 1798. In the case of the bicentenary, in marked contrast to the past, the cross-community and inclusive nature of the commemorations, north and south, has been most heartening. Throughout this work, I have attempted to observe, compare and contrast the commemorative process in all its aspects.

PETER COLLINS
JANUARY 2004

1

The Contest of Memory –
the Nineteenth Century

THE SOCIETY OF UNITED IRISHMEN itself, to an extent, originated in commemoration. When it was founded in Belfast in October 1791, many of its members and supporters had been energised by the enthusiastic and widespread second anniversary commemorations of the fall of the Bastille, held the previous July. The same radical enthusiasm was generated by the Bastille Day celebrations in Belfast and Dublin in 1792. For the United Irishmen these commemorations were both a propaganda exercise and a means of establishing an affinity with the French Revolution, which in many respects they sought to emulate. In much the same way, since the 1798 Rising, many groups, during successive periods of commemoration, have sought to establish such an affinity with the United Irishmen.

The aim of this work is to identify these many authors of commemoration and to analyse their often competing motivations. As we shall see, for some, commemoration simply aimed at rekindling interest in the United Irish principles of Liberty, Equality and Fraternity, and establishing a Brotherhood of Affection between Protestant, Catholic and Dissenter. Advanced Republicans also used the United Irish memory to further their radical separatist project. Others, while hostile to the separatist, secular, revolutionary Republicanism of the United Irishmen, got involved in commemoration due to pragmatic political necessities of their own day. Thus the Catholic Church, by the time of the centenary, played a role in the popular programme of '98 commemoration although it had virulently opposed the United Irishmen in the 1790s. This was largely intended to mitigate the much more radical agenda of the Irish Republican Brotherhood (IRB). The Church successfully imposed its 'Faith and Fatherland' version of '98 on the centenary commemorations, overwhelming the revolutionary secular interpretation of the Fenians. Constitutional Nationalists, at first wary of commemorating a failed physical-force revolution, were also forced to get involved in 1898 to avoid leaving the field to their Republican opponents.

How and why the legacy of the United Irishmen has continued to impact on politics down the generations is well put by Kevin Whelan:

> The 1798 rebellion was fought twice: once on the battlefields and then in the war of words which followed in those bloody footprints. The struggle for the control of the meaning of the 1790s was also a struggle for political legitimacy, and the high drama of the union debate was dominated by discussion of 1798. The interpretation of 1798 was designed to mould public opinion and influence policy formation: the rebellion never passed into history because it never passed out of politics.[1]

It is equally important here to seek to interpret and understand why many in Ireland were opposed to the project of, and the commemoration of, the United Irishmen. In particular, the hostile attitude of Loyalists to commemoration of the Rising of 1798 must be explained. Although many Loyalists, particularly Presbyterians in the north, were descendants of the United Irishmen, by the time of the centenary – and indeed much earlier – they had become implacably opposed to the United Irish project and its commemoration.

Aftershock

Even before the Rising, the ruthless 'Dragooning of Ulster' by General Lake, a whirlwind of arms seizures, hangings, pitch-cappings and other tortures, had seared the collective psyche of many Presbyterians and others in the province. This was so extensive that many who sympathised failed to turn out in 1798. In the immediate aftermath of '98, there was a collective recoil from the shock of the disastrous events which, in only a few months, had led to some 30,000 deaths and the maiming, gaoling and exile of many thousands more. Hardly a family in certain areas in Ireland was left untouched.

For various reasons, many sought to distance themselves from the Rising. A form of collective amnesia occurred, particularly in Counties Antrim and Down. Many Presbyterians either were ashamed of, or sought to cover for, relatives who had died as rebels or were in captivity or on the run. Thus, it is said, some gravestones were marked 'died June 1797' or 'died June 1799' although the deceased had actually been killed in June 1798. In at least one case, a family held a bogus funeral for a hunted member who had escaped to America.

The representative body for most Presbyterians was the Synod of Ulster. It was worried by the Presbyterian complexion of the Rising in Ulster.[2] The Synod had been deeply traumatised by the public hanging of the Rev. James Porter in front of his church at Greyabbey. It was further scandalised by the reports that some of its clergy had assumed a leadership role in the United Irishmen. Prominent among these were Robert Acheson, Samuel Barber, Thomas Ledlie Birch, William Steel Dickson, Sinclare Kelburne, and Archibald Warwick. Furthermore, the Synod needed to distance itself and its clergy from the Rising for a very practical reason. This was the regium donum, a Government stipend to Presbyterian clergy which, especially after the Rising, was selectively doled out to those whose loyalty was beyond question.

Consequently, the Synod held an inquiry into the conduct of its ministers and probationers and found that only a small number were involved. Rev. William Steel Dickson on his return from imprisonment without trial in Fort George in Scotland was excluded from the regium donum. He was readmitted to the Synod despite the objections of many. Like Banquo's ghost, he remained as a reproach to the new order in the Synod, railing against 'the pious and loyal servility of a small, but, latterly, a dominant party'.[3] The majority view within the Synod that the Rising was unjustified was expressed in a pastoral address:

> Did not every Christian denomination enjoy perfect liberty of conscience? Were not the shackles broken which had confined our trade? Was not private property secure, and the land every day becoming more prosperous? [4]

Soon after the Rising, the various factions began to put 'spin' on what had happened. This often amounted to deliberate obfuscation. Indeed, many United Irish survivors, attempting to extricate themselves from danger, began to muddy the waters by leaving a

trail of self-justification or by underplaying the roles of themselves
or their comrades. Frequently, they portrayed themselves as having
initially followed the path of constitutional reform, only subsequently being sucked unwillingly into the rising as a response to
either deliberate Loyalist provocation or repression by the
Government. In another scenario, the Society of United Irishmen
was portrayed as only marginally involved in Wexford, which was
shown as essentially a Jacquerie led by Catholic priests.[5] Such views
were countered in the accounts of radicals such as Samuel Neilson,
particularly United Irish émigrés in America, who maintained that
all phases of the rebellion north, south and west resulted from the
deliberate revolutionary strategy of the United Irishmen. Hostile
explications were also refuted in the memoirs of the United Irish
veteran Jemmy Hope, published in the middle of the nineteenth
century. These arguments would continue to be rehearsed in later
years, particularly during anniversary commemorations of the 1798
rising.

Loyalists

The seminal Loyalist version of '98 was set down in Sir Richard
Musgrave's highly partisan *Memoirs of the Various Rebellions*
(Dublin, 1801). In style, content and purpose, this was the equivalent of Temple's accounts of the 1641 massacres in Ireland. It was
based on answers to a questionnaire that Musgrave sent to Loyalist
gentry and clergy, framed in a leading way, about their experiences
in 1798. Musgrave, whose main purpose was to present the Irish
Loyalist case to an English audience, made the link between 1641,
1690 and 1798, portraying each as a successive phase in the
Catholic campaign to overthrow Protestant hegemony in Ireland.
For good measure, he made further connections with the twelfth-
century papal crusades against the Albigensians and Waldensians
and the sixteenth-century St Bartholomew's Day massacre of
French Huguenots. Musgrave drew a distinction between the phases of the Rising in Wexford and Ulster. He portrayed the former
as a 'sectarian', priest-led, peasant rising, whereas in the latter
misguided Presbyterians, disaffected by the burden of tithes and

rack-rent, were led into rebellion by disloyal rabble-rousers. To make his point, he highlighted, in very colourful language, atrocities in Wexford such as the barn-burning tragedy at Scullabogue.

Musgrave's book was the first major account of the rebellion and set the agenda for Loyalist interpretations of '98 for many generations. Also, in its own time, it played a major part in the propaganda war being waged against the Act of Union, which Musgrave and many Irish Loyalists and Orangemen had opposed. They feared that the demise of the Irish parliament would replace their careful control of the country with that of Englishmen who were either disinterested in or hostile to the Irish Protestant cause. They believed that this was already happening in what they regarded as appeasement policies of the Viceroy Cornwallis towards the defeated United Irishmen and the Catholic Church. Loyalists stressed the need instead for vigorous pre-emptive policies to avoid a repetition of 1798.

Musgrave and his fellow Loyalists were concerned to support the position of the Established Church and were especially opposed to Catholic Emancipation, which was initially contained in the proposed package for legislative Union with Britain. Furthermore, they sought to bring 'misled' Presbyterians into the Protestant Loyalist fold, in order to present a united front to future Catholic and radical assaults on the political *status quo*. The 1798 rebellion, though already part of history, was continuing to have an impact on politics. Down the years this would continue to be the case.

The Catholic Church
and the aftermath of 1798

Archbishop Troy of Dublin was concerned to distance the Catholic Church from the rebellion. Firstly, given the reprisals that immediately followed, including church burnings in Wexford, he naturally sought to mitigate the Loyalist backlash against the members and property of his Church. Troy was also concerned that the good relations between the Catholic Church and the Government, carefully nurtured since the winding-down of the Penal Laws, should continue. These had brought gains such as the Catholic Relief Act of

1793 and Maynooth College, founded in 1795 under the auspices of the Government. Furthermore, the Hierarchy supported the Union, believing that it would deliver them from the anti-Catholic elements in the Irish parliament. In addition, they welcomed the accompanying measure of Catholic Emancipation initially promised by the Government. Most of all, the Catholic Church had opposed the revolutionary United Irishmen because, if successful, they would have introduced a secular republic on the model of their French ally. If this had happened, the Hierarchy feared a similar fate to that which had befallen the Church in revolutionary France. They were also worried that polemicists like Musgrave, who were working hard to detach Government from its rapprochement with the Catholic Hierarchy, might be successful.

In 1798, the Hierarchy had acted quickly to warn their flock against following the path of rebellion. On the Sunday after Father Murphy had taken the field, the following circular letter was sent to the priests of the Archdiocese of Dublin:

Dearest Brethren,

In the present awful and alarming period when every good subject, every good Christian views with grief and horror the desperate and wicked endeavours of irreligious and rebellious agitators to overturn and destroy the constitution, we should deem ourselves criminal in the sight of God did we not, in the most solemn and impressive manner, remind you of the heinousness of violating the laws of our country and of oath.

Let no one deceive you by wretched impracticable speculations on the rights of man and the majesty of the people; on the dignity and independence of the human mind; on the abstract duties of superiors and exaggerated abuses of authority – fatal speculations, disastrous theories not more subversive of social order and happiness than destructive of principle of the Christian religion ... submission to established authority and obedience to the laws are amongst the duties prescribed by religion; every violation of these duties is highly criminal. Wherefore if any amongst you have been unfortunately seduced into a combination against the state ... without this sincere sorrow and amendment you cannot expect

absolution in the tribunal of penance nor mercy from Government
... Resolve then we beseech you to deliver up your arms ... unite
with all your loyal and peaceable fellow subjects to crush the
wicked spirit of insurrection.

JOHN TROY[6]
Archbishop of Dublin

This pronouncement was published in the Dublin newspapers the
following day (upon which Father Murphy gained his first victory),
and was signed by every Catholic archbishop and bishop in Ireland,
with the sole exception of Bishop Hussey of Waterford. Priests who
favoured the rebels were suspended from the performance of their
religious duties, and James Caulfield, Bishop of Ferns, recorded that
while Wexford town was in the hands of the British troops, it was
crowded with priests who had fled before the rebels.[7]

After the Rising, the difficulty for the Hierarchy was to explain
away the involvement of a small number of priests – such as Fathers
John and Michael Murphy – in a leadership capacity in the rebellion in Wexford. Archbishop Troy, wishing to protect the position
of the Church, expressed his fears on this issue: 'We all wish to
remain as we are and we would so were it not that too many of the
clergy were active in the wicked rebellion or did not oppose it.'[8]
Furthermore, in Troy's view, the Rising in Wexford was 'purely self-
defence by Catholic peasants against sectarian attacks' and not part
of a United Irish orchestrated campaign.[9]

Dr Caulfield, in whose diocese Wexford lay, had most to fear in
terms of retaliation. He was in Wexford town during its occupation
by the rebels, and sought to distance both himself and the majority of the clergy of his diocese from the Rising. Caulfield anathema-
tised the few Wexford priests who did participate in the Rising as,
'Excommunicated priests, drunken and profligate couple-beggars –
the very faeces of the church'.[10] He was at one with Troy in striving
to keep open the Church's links to the Government:

> I am persuaded in my own mind we shall be better off than ever if
> the ruling powers are convinced that the late unfortunate wicked
> rising was not on the part of Catholics a rebellion against the king
> but against the Protestant ascendancy and Orangemen.[11]

Daniel O'Connell,
Catholic Nationalism and
the lost memory of '98

Catholic retreat from the memory of the 1798 rising wasn't confined to the clergy. In the eighteenth century the Protestant political élite, which controlled the Irish parliament, had defined the nation in terms of themselves alone. The United Irishmen had sought to negate this by substituting the common name of 'Irishman' for Protestant, Catholic and Dissenter. From the 1820s, the emerging political leadership of Daniel O'Connell was posited largely on separate deals with Government, on behalf of the Catholics of Ireland, within the existing political system. He followed up his successful campaign for Catholic Emancipation with the unsuccessful Repeal agitation aimed at recreating an Irish parliament, this time with an inbuilt Catholic majority. Effectively this meant forging a synthesis between Catholicism and Nationalism – a further narrowing of the definition of the Irish Nation.

In pursuit of his political aims, O'Connell sought to distance himself from revolutionary Nationalism. He was, as is well known, riddled with contradictions. His own version of his activities in 1798 was that as a member of the Dublin Lawyers' Yeomanry he had opposed the Rebellion. Whelan cites the testimony of Francis Higgins, the Dublin Castle spymaster, that O'Connell had been a United Irishman but had escaped the consequences and subsequently distanced himself from involvement.[12] O'Connell was repelled by the violence of 'the Terror' that he had witnessed firsthand in France during the Revolution. He advocated solely constitutionalist politics, and eschewed violence to the extent of backing down in the face of a Government ban on the 'monster meeting' called at Clontarf in 1843. Ironically, he had killed an opponent, Norcot d'Esterre, in a duel fought in 1815, though he was so horrified by its outcome that he repudiated all violence from that time.

O'Connell's nationalism later became largely Catholic, with little or no place for Protestants. Furthermore, he denied that Catholics and Protestants had made common cause in 1798. In 1825, when asked if there were any Catholics among the United Irishmen, he replied:

There were scarcely any among the leading United Irishmen who were almost all Dissenters. In the North, the lower classes of United Irishmen were at first Dissenters; it spread then among the Roman Catholics and as it spread into the southern counties, and took in the population, it increased its number of Catholics. In the county of Wexford, where the greatest part of the rebellion raged, there were no United Irishmen previous to the rebellion and there would have been no rebellion there if they had not been forced forwards by the establishment of Orange lodges and the whippings and torturings and things of that kind.[13]

O'Connell's view was that Catholics had been used by self-seeking Presbyterians to extract further parliamentary reform for their own benefit. As a consequence, the Catholics had borne the brunt of brutal repression as a result of a rebellion of which they were not the authors. By May 1841, O'Connell's line had hardened further:

As to 1798, we leave the weak and wicked men who considered sanguinary violence as part of their resources for ameliorating our institutions, and the equally wicked and villainously designing wretches who fomented the rebellion, and made it explode in order that in the defeat of the rebellious attempt, they might be able to extinguish the liberties of Ireland. We leave both these classes of miscreants to the contempt and indignation of mankind.[14]

Furthermore, O'Connell, with a cavalier disregard of the facts, was particularly contemptuous of Ulster Presbyterians:

The Presbyterians fought badly at Ballynahinch – they were commanded there by one Dickie, an attorney, and as soon as these fellows were checked, they became furious Orangemen and have continued so ever since.[15]

Presbyterian sea-change

As we have seen, many Presbyterians began to disengage from the United Irish project very soon after the failure of the Rising of 1798. Stories of sectarian atrocities against Protestants in Wexford, such as the Scullabogue massacre, also had an effect. Many

Presbyterians had originally accepted Tone's *Argument on Behalf of the Catholics of Ireland* (1791), in which he cited the ability of revolutionary Catholic France to throw off Papal domination, expressing the hope that the case would be similar in a post-revolution Ireland. The Concordat concluded between Napoleon and the Pope in 1804 seemed finally to dash these hopes. O'Connell's activities were also a major factor in weaning many Presbyterians from their earlier *rapprochement* with Catholics. Undoubtedly O'Connell's introduction of Emancipation and Repeal into the political equation frightened many Presbyterians into a new pan-Protestant alliance. The 'Liberator' went north only rarely, his visits attended by controversy and conflict. The Irish political landscape was increasingly polarised, with sectarian fault-lines opening up between north and south and also within Ulster in particular.

Ironically, O'Connell's status of 'bogeyman' for Protestants proved useful for his Presbyterian arch-foe, Henry Cooke. Cooke's project was to wean Presbyterians away from adherence to liberal ideals in both politics and theology. He had been baptised by a radical Presbyterian minister and had grown up in the bosom of a liberal congregation in Maghera, Co Derry.[16] As a youth, Cooke had witnessed the burning by the Tipperary Militia of his meeting-house and other outrages during the 1798 rebellion. This confirmed him in his political and religious conservatism. He became the leading advocate of the majority orthodox tendency of Presbyterianism known as 'Old Light'.

Cooke became involved in a struggle for the hearts and minds of Ulster Presbyterians against the 'New Light' liberal strain led by Rev. Henry Montgomery. Two of Montgomery's brothers had been in the 'turn-out' at Antrim, and his house had been looted and burned by the yeomanry. Though opposed to insurrection, he was radical in politics and a supporter of Catholic Emancipation. He was one of the few supporters of Steel Dickson in the Synod.

The theological and political debates between the two divines were inextricably linked. The theological controversy centred on subscription to the Westminster Confession of Faith and the Unitarian views of the 'New Light'. The 'New Light' were stigmatised by Cooke as 'Arians'.[17] Cooke came out the eventual winner, if not in argument then certainly in terms of the numbers adhering to his theology. Most 'New Light' congregations were eventually subsumed into the Non-Subscribing Presbyterian Church, which today embodies (though not exclusively) liberal Presbyterianism. A leading church in this tradition is Rosemary Street Presbyterian, Belfast, where the United Irish ideologue Dr William Drennan's father had been minister.

Cooke and his supporters portrayed the majority of Presbyterians who had been in the 'turn-out' in 1798 as of the 'New Light' persuasion. There were many such, but the participation of a multitude of orthodox Presbyterians including clergy is beyond dispute.[18]

Cooke's vivid invocation of the memory of the Loyalist Protestant victims in Wexford led to many Presbyterians turning away from their former United Irish adherence:

> The unhappy men and women who fell victims at Scullabogue barn and Wexford Bridge have been the political saviours of their country. They live in our remembrance. Their deaths opened the eyes of many thousands in Ulster.[19]

In 1834, at a meeting in Hillsborough called to cement the political union of all Protestants in the face of O'Connell's Catholic Nationalism, Cooke proclaimed the 'banns of marriage' between the Presbyterian and Established Churches. The Orange Order, which now opened the doors of its lodges to Presbyterians, became the cement holding this new entente in place.[20] Effectively, this conservative political and theological realignment spelled the end of the Brotherhood of Affection so central to the United Irish project. Nevertheless, Cooke was seen by many Presbyterians – even clergy who supported him theologically in the Synod – as being on the side of the Conservative, Ascendancy and landlord class, the traditional oppressors of Ulster Presbyterians.

By the late 1820s, many northern Presbyterians were prospering under the Act of Union. They had been glad to see the back of the old Irish parliament, in which they had little or no representation. While many Presbyterians supported Catholic Emancipation, they were mainly against Repeal. The fear was that a Dublin parliament, controlled by the Catholic Nationalist supporters of O'Connell, would result in Presbyterians again being politically disenfranchised and would wreck their new-found prosperity.

This realignment among Presbyterians was a gradual process, and no doubt proceeded at a different tempo in different areas. An interesting illustration of how this happened in one local area is contained in the following account of developments in Greyabbey, Co Down:

> The political viewpoint of those who had turned out in '98 did not change overnight. While most regretted the loss of life and property that had occurred, they still favoured the radical political programme, without showing the least desire to take up arms to promote their aims. After 1800 the cry of parliamentary reform was silenced by the abolition of the hated ascendancy parliament and an end to its more dubious proceedings, when Castlereagh famously bought out forever 'the fee simple of Irish corruption'. From then on the administration, if all too slowly, could afford to turn its attention to creating a juster system ... In places such as Newtownards, Greyabbey and Conlig, that 'rebel shuttle row', the defiant spirit of '98 lingered on, although increasingly the pursuit of a minority among the working class weavers, known as the 'Greenmen', North Down's reply to the growing strength of Orangeism which did not gain a secure foothold in the area until the Emancipation crisis. Greyabbey witnessed an ugly Orange versus Green riot in 1829, leading to the conviction of four Orangemen, presumably during the heightened feelings of the emancipation agitation, although the petitioning mania both for and against emancipation in North Down would indicate a fairly strong majority against the measure. By 1838 the Orangemen had the Greyabbey Greens on the defensive and the 1860s saw the formation of an Orange lodge in the village, significantly entitled 'Unexpected No Surrender'.
>
> During the hard-fought County election of 1852 Newtownards Greenmen could still summon up enough spirit to raise a Green arch in Mary St., in reply to the six Orange arches about the town and the last recorded fight took place at the Cottown on the Twelfth of that year, which the Orangemen of Donaghadee celebrated in a rather bad ballad. The '98 tradition may be said to have passed away with Jemmy Cavan, 'the last of the croppies', who was

a young servant boy to Patrick Wightman in 1798. Cavan died in 1872, by which time Orangeism was much more attuned to Presbyterian concerns. The town was the venue for William Johnston's famous Orange walk to Bangor in 1867. Every Twelfth Cavan would wear orange lilies on his coat tails, and presumably was regarded as a curiosity surviving from an earlier, now forgotten age.[21]

Nevertheless, the strain of liberal Presbyterianism did not die out; for example, many Presbyterians were involved in the tenant rights movement in the years after the Famine. Rather it had been transformed into something akin to the Liberalism then emerging in Britain. In the process it did not lose touch with its turbulent past. This is vividly described by the editor of the liberal *Northern Whig*, Thomas McKnight. Looking back on the 1860s, he recalled:

> The Protestant liberals of Ulster, whose fathers and grandfathers were United Irishmen, had generally become warm supporters of the liberal party as it had been led by Charles Grey, Lord Melbourne, Lord John Russell and recently by Lord Palmerston. Though the descendants of the United Irishmen they were not at all disposed themselves to become rebels; but they were rather proud of their ancestors for having been rebels. The events of that time, two years before the Act of Union, were vividly present to the descendants of those who had suffered in that dreadful resurrection, or series of resurrections. The wounds, though healed, left scars still visible. The scenes of the battles, as at Ballynahinch, and of the executions, as of McCracken in Belfast, were still pointed out.[22]

As will be seen further on, despite an uneasy alliance with the Conservatives later in the century to confront Home Rule, liberal Presbyterianism and radical principles continued to be a force in Ulster politics right up to the crisis in the years prior to the First World War.[23]

Mid-nineteenth-century religious antipathy

In the middle of the nineteenth century, relations between

Catholicism and Protestantism hit a new low. Ultramontanism, as expounded by Pope Pius IX, was an assertion of more direct control by Rome over the Church throughout the world. It also manifested in a growth of hostility towards other branches of Christianity. Indeed, Protestants in Ireland were well aware of the persecution of their co-religionists in some Catholic countries in Europe. The Church appeared to be lined up with the forces of reaction. The publication of the Syllabus of Errors in the 1860s – a catalogue of the 'errors of modernism' such as Liberalism and Socialism – for many showed the drift of the Church in a more intransigent direction. The culmination of this trend was the declaration of Papal Infallibility, which was deeply resented in Protestant circles. It led in Germany to the Kulturkampf – the struggle between the state led by Bismarck and the Catholic Church. Even Gladstone reacted negatively to this movement by the papacy.

The rector of the Irish College in Rome, Paul Cullen, who was closely associated with Pius IX, was sent to Ireland as its first cardinal with the aim of bringing the Church here into line with the ultramontanist tendency. Under his influence a 'Devotional Revolution' ensued, producing a more hard-line, intolerant and, to many Protestants, triumphalist Church. The Catholic Church in Ireland became better organised, more effective and proactive in social issues. Its increasing confidence was reflected throughout Ireland in the spate of church-building and the arrival of religious orders from the Continent.

While Irish Protestants looked askance at these developments, there was a mirror image in an increasingly evangelical trend in Protestantism. This swept from America through Britain, Ireland and Europe, culminating in the so-called 'Great Awakening' of 1859. The result was that many came under the influence of a hard-line fundamentalist and intolerant strain of Protestantism. These attitudinal shifts resulted in a religious cold war between Protestants and Catholics, exacerbated in Ireland by deepening political divisions. Even liberal Protestants became more suspicious and fearful of their Catholic neighbours, believing them to be priest-ridden and not worthy of sharing political power. This was the antithesis of the aspirations of the United Irishmen.

The myth-making continues

Against this backdrop, the sectarian interpretation of '98 by Musgrave and other Loyalist propagandists flourished. As we shall see later, this was mirrored by an equal travesty of the memory of the United Irishmen and the events of '98 on the Catholic side. The myth-making continued with George Cruickshank's hostile and grotesque cartoons in W.H. Maxwell's *History of the 1798 Rebellion in Ireland* (London, 1845). Cruickshank, famous as an illustrator of the works of Charles Dickens, produced one-sided illustrations of 1798. His shocking depictions of the piking of prisoners at Wexford Bridge and the burning barn at Scullabogue had much the same resonance and impact as the lurid and exaggerated pamphlets and cartoons of the seventeenth century. Portraying the atrocities of the 1641 Rising, such as the massacre at Portadown Bridge, these had been used as propaganda and justification for Cromwell's subsequent campaign in Ireland. Cruickshank's simian and racist characterisations of the Irish were aped in *Punch* and other journals. Sir John Tenniel (the illustrator of *Alice in Wonderland*) specialised in nasty stereotypes of Irish peasants, particularly in relation to the activities of the Fenians.

Recovering the memory of the United Irishmen

From this low point the memory of the United Irishmen experienced rehabilitation due to the memoirs of veterans of the movement, in tandem with the works of Dr R.R. Madden. Madden's *United Irishmen, Their Life and Times* (London, 1842–7), published in several volumes, verged on hagiography. He was a conservative Catholic who was opposed equally to tyranny and revolution; nor had he any time for the utopianism that characterised the more advanced United Irishmen. Madden's work, in part, was a cautionary tale of the consequences of misrule, which he meant as a lesson for the Government of his day. He didn't distinguish between the democrats and the revolutionaries, nor between United Irish political aims and the Catholic interest. Madden used questionnaire and letter to interview some 50 surviving, mostly second-ranking, United Irishmen. He encouraged Jemmy Hope to write his *Autobiography of a Working Man*, and included it in the third edition of his own book.[24] In this, in answer to the criticism of the United Irish project, Hope wrote:

> It is hard for a man who did not live at the time to believe or comprehend the extent to which misrepresentations were carried at the close of our struggle: for besides the paid agents the men who flinched and fell away from our cause grasped at any apology for their own delinquency.[25]

One of Madden's informants was Mary Ann McCracken, sister of Henry Joy and in her own right a living personification of the liberal political and social principles of the United Irishmen. Unaccountably, Madden didn't interview Tone's widow Matilda, then still alive in America. Madden's book had a tremendous impact both in reviving interest in the United Irishmen and in reinstating their reputation, primarily in Nationalist quarters. Indeed, Maxwell's book had been published as a Loyalist riposte to Madden.

'98 in song and verse

In the 1840s, the works of Madden and Hope had an influence on the emerging Young Ireland movement. The popular Irish melodies of Tom Moore provided mood music in heightening popular support for the Young Irelanders, as well as providing lasting remembrance of the United Irishmen. A good example was 'Sarah Curran' (also known as 'She is Far From the Land'). This portrays the anguish of an Irish exile, Sarah Curran, mourning her glamorous patriot lover Robert Emmet. After he was captured during the abortive postscript to '98, her unsigned letters were found in Emmet's coat. Curran, the daughter of the famous lawyer John Philpot Curran, was driven from her home by the anger of her compromised father. Having fled to Cork she met a soldier, Robert Sturgeon, whom she married and accompanied to Sicily. She never got over Emmet, and it was this heady cocktail of lost love, martyrdom, and exile that captured the public imagination. Moore's song, written at a time of great disillusionment, in many respects also reflects the mourning of Nationalist Ireland for the loss of the romantic young patriot Emmet.

SARAH CURRAN

She is far from the land where her young hero sleeps
And lovers around her are sighing;
But coldly she turns from their gaze and weeps
For her heart in his grave is lying.

She sings the wild songs of her dear native plain
Every note which he loved awaking;
Ah! Little they think, who delight in her strains,
How the heart of her minstrel is breaking

He had lived for his love, for his country he died
They were all that to life had entwined him;
Nor soon shall the tears of his country be dried,
Nor long will his love stay behind him.

Oh! Make her a grave where the sunbeams rest
When they promise a glorious morrow;
They'll shine o'er her sleep, like a smile from the west
From her own loved island of sorrow.

'The Croppy Boy', written by W.B. McBurney (a.k.a. Carroll Malone) was first published in the Young Ireland newspaper *The Nation* in 1845. The term 'croppy' refers to the short hair-styles adopted by the rebels in sympathy with revolutionary France, where cropped hair was a badge of radicalism. Based on anecdote, the story was included in *The Sham Squire* by W.J. Fitzpatrick. In it a youth, on his way to the Battle of Oulart in 1798, calls to a church to beg absolution prior to the battle. He discloses his war-like intentions in confession to a man that in fact is a captain of the Yeomanry, impersonating the priest. The soldier throws off the soutane, revealing his red uniform, and arrests the youth, who is subsequently shot. Such patriotic melodrama held a great deal of appeal for much of the readership of *The Nation*:

At the siege of Ross did my father fall,
And at Gorey my loving brothers all,
I alone am left of my name and race
I will go to Wexford and take their place ...

The priest said naught, but a rustling noise
Made the youth look up in wild surprise:
The robes came off, and in scarlet there
Sat a yeoman captain with fiery glare

With fiery glare and with fury hoarse,
Instead of a blessing he breathed a curse:
'Twas a good thought, boy to come here and shrive
For one short hour is your time to live ...

'The Memory of the Dead'

Of utmost importance in rekindling interest in '98, in this period
and subsequently, was 'The Memory of the Dead' (known popu-
larly by its first line, 'Who Fears to Speak of '98?'). In 1843, John
Kells Ingram penned 'The Memory of the Dead' while he was a stu-
dent at Trinity College Dublin. It was first published anonymously
in the *The Nation* on 1 April 1843. Set to music, probably by
William Elliot Hudson, it was first performed as a song on St
Patrick's Day 1843. It became the anthem of subsequent '98 commemorations.

THE MEMORY OF THE DEAD

Who fears to speak of Ninety-Eight?
Who blushes at the name?
When cowards mock the patriot's fate,
Who hangs his head for shame?
He's all a knave and half a slave
Who slights his country thus,
But a true man, like you, man,
Will fill your glass with us

We drink the memory of the brave
The faithful and the few
Some lie far off beyond the wave,
Some sleep in Ireland too;
All, all are gone; but still lives on
The fame of those who died
All true men, like you men
Remember them with pride.[26]

Ingram later became a member of the academic establishment, drawing from O'Connell the sneering reproof, 'The bird that once sang so sweetly is now caged within the walls of Trinity College.'

An article appeared in the *Irish News* at the time of the 150th anniversary of '98, which throws much light on Kells Ingram and his anthem. It is worth quoting in full:

'The Memory of the Dead'

J.R. McKEOWN

Out of all the songs inspired by the Insurrection of '98 none has lingered in the popular mind as 'The Memory of the Dead.' (Maybe readers will know it better as 'Who Fears to Speak of Ninety-Eight,' which are the words of its opening line, but to so call it is to confuse it with one of that title by Lionel Johnson.) It has been sung and recited thousands of times in all parts of the world where Irishmen have gathered, and it is not unlikely, indeed, that when all the scholastic achievements of its distinguished author are long forgotten he will be still remembered by this famous song alone. Strangely enough, it was not until more than forty years after the Rising that the famous ballad was written. More strange still, perhaps – and maybe so much the more tribute to its author and the epoch which inspired him – the man who wrote it was not even born for more than twenty years after the 'dark and evil days' which it recalls. It is, perhaps, appropriate that John Kells Ingram, its author, should have had close associations with the North where the seeds of '98 were sown. Son of a Protestant clergyman, he was born on 7th July 1823, near Pettigo, County Donegal. His father, for what reason does not seem apparent, sent him to Newry for his early education, and at the age of 14 he entered Trinity College. To say that he remained there for some 60 years is not to suggest any dullness or inattention to his studies, for in the interim he held several of its important professorships and for a long period was Vice-Provost of the University. Of a reputedly retiring disposition, Ingram was regarded as one of the greatest scholars of his age. His contributions to literature included a History of Political Economy translated into no fewer than nine European languages as well as Japanese.

It will be well to remember here that Ingram was not a Young Irelander. 'I never was a member of the group,' he wrote in 1900, 'but some of them were known to me and I had one dear friend amongst them, John (afterwards Judge) O'Hagan.' He was, however, associated with many of the learned and progressive societies of his day, notably the College Historical Society (whose membership has from time to time included so many well-remembered Irishmen) and the Royal Irish Academy. For several years prior to his death he had been a Trustee of the National Library, and was one of the Commissioners appointed to revise the Brehon Laws.

It is not however, so much with his scholastic and, public eminence that we are at present concerned, but with his 'Memory of the Dead'. One evening, it is related he was entertaining three fellow-students (subsequently ordained to the Protestant ministry) and their discussions turned on the '98 Rising. Apparently inspiration came suddenly to Ingram, for it is recorded that he left his friends to their talk while he retired to his bedroom. After working on it all night the poem was next evening dropped at *The Nation* office. It appeared in that famous paper on the 1st April, 1843 (unsigned) and almost immediately attracted attention. Since then it has held its place as perhaps the most popular of all the ballads and songs written around the United Irishmen and their period.

The poem subsequently appeared over the author's name in 'The Spirit of the Nation'– a collection gathered from the columns of the paper. It was translated into Latin by Robert Yelverton Tyrell and into Irish by Dr Douglas Hyde and others. And it won a new and extensive popularity during the '98 centenary celebrations of 50 years ago, when its author was still alive for he did not die until so comparatively recently as 1907.

In the years subsequent to its publication, when he had become a staunch Unionist, it was hinted that Ingram was ashamed of his poem and would have repudiated its authorship. To this he gave the lie himself by including it in a collection of 'Sonnets and Other

Poems' which he published in 1900. In a note to this collection he wrote: '"The Memory of the Dead" was my only contribution to *The Nation* ... I have reproduced it here ... because some persons have believed, or affected to believe, that I am ashamed of having written it, and would gladly, if I could, disclaim its authorship. Those who know me need not be told that this idea is without foundation.'

The Toast

In the same note he gave us this hint that even though he had become Unionist he was not at least anti-Irish. 'I think the Irish race should be grateful to the men who in other times, however mistaken may have been their policy, gave their lives for their country.' That his belief was restricted, however, by the qualification which we have emphasised, suggests that he was out of sympathy with the more revolutionary movements of his later days, and so, almost certainly he was – for what Unionist was not? For all that, he is due our gratitude for his moving lines of tribute to the men of '98. They deserve and he has given us the toast ...[27]

Young Ireland and 1848

Some in Young Ireland saw themselves as standing in a kind of Apostolic Succession to the United Irishmen. Thomas Davis (1814–45) was assiduous in recovering the memory and reputation of the United Irishmen and devoted much space to them in the columns of *The Nation*. Young Ireland's aim was to roll back the O'Connellite tide of Catholic Nationalism and resurrect the United Irish project of uniting Protestant, Catholic and Dissenter. Davis was engaged in a biography of Wolfe Tone when his own life was cut short. Already he had made Tone's grave the focal point of commemoration and homage. Madden, in 1842, had authoritatively identified the grave of the patriot at Bodenstown. Davis' poem 'Tone's Grave', published in *The Nation* on 25 November 1843, is a clarion call for commemoration.

TONE'S GRAVE

In Bodenstown Churchyard there is a green grave
And wildly around it the winter winds rave
Small shelter, I ween, are the ruined walls there
When the storm sweeps down, on the plains of Kildare

Once I lay on that sod – it lies over Wolfe Tone
And thought how he perished in prison alone
His friends unavenged, and his country unfreed
'Oh bitter!' I said, 'Is the patriot's mead'

But the old man who saw I was mourning there said
'We come Sir to weep where young Wolfe Tone is laid
and we're going to raise him a monument too –
a plain one, yet fit for the simple and true"

My heart overflowed, and I clasped his old hand
And I blessed him and blessed every one of this band;
'Sweet sweet, 'tis to find that such faith can remain
To the cause and the man so long vanquished and slain'

In Bodenstown Churchyard there is a green grave
And freely around it, let winter winds rave
Far better they suit him, the ruin and the gloom
Till Ireland, a nation, can build him a Tomb

Davis sought to erect a headstone at the grave of Tone. However, O'Connell's lieutenants, particularly his counsel, feared that such an act of defiance would be to the Liberator's detriment at his ongoing state trial. The Young Irelanders did erect a black marble slab at Bodenstown in 1844, though without ceremony, in order not to embarrass O'Connell in his relations with the Government. This was an indication that the memory of the dead of '98 was still capable of provoking controversy.

Nevertheless, the Young Irelanders were not always to be so considerate of the Liberator's position. Although Young Ireland leaders such as William Smith O'Brien supported the aims of the United Irishmen, initially they tried to reject the physical force tactics that

had been so disastrous in 1798. The logic of their later refutation of
O'Connell's Catholic constitutional Nationalism was the somewhat
tragicomic rising of 1848, itself surely the utmost manifestation of
commemoration of the United Irishmen and identification with
'98. John Mitchel, son of a Presbyterian minister from Newry, who
deliberately chose *The United Irishman* as the title of his newspaper,
was the most ardent advocate of physical force in Young Ireland.
F.S.L. Lyons shows how Mitchell kept the flame of revolutionary
republicanism burning and ultimately passed on the torch:

> Mitchell looked back to Wolfe Tone and this was his central sig-
> nificance in the movement, for in doing so he linked the dispirit-
> ed and famished Ireland of his own day with the most formidable
> uprising in modern Irish history and through it with the fountain-
> head of the republican tradition. Of course Mitchell did more than
> look back to the past, he held a lesson for the future as well, a les-
> son absorbed equally by the Fenians in 1867 and by Connolly and
> Pearse in 1916.[28]

The Young Irelanders had attempted to rekindle the United Irish
project of an alliance between Protestant, Catholic and Dissenter,
leading to a secular republic. However, the timing was inauspicious
due to the Great Famine and growing divisions in the country.
Catholics – many of whom viewed the Famine as an attempt at
genocide by the Government – resented their political and economic impotence, not least over the question of land ownership.
Protestants feared the loss of political and religious liberty and economic well-being that they believed would ensue if Ireland severed
the link with Britain. Due to the Famine and the failure of the 1848
rising, there was no cause for celebration, no time for a 50th
anniversary commemoration.

Myles Byrne

Another important figure in recovering the memory of the United
Irishmen was Myles Byrne, a veteran both of '98 and of the Emmet
sequel of 1803. He had gone into exile in France, where he became
a distinguished soldier. He kept in touch with Irish politics, and was
Paris correspondent of *The Nation*. His memoirs, dictated in old

age to his wife, were published posthumously in 1863 and had a deep impact in Ireland. Byrne's importance was that, as an eye-witness and participant, he could refute comprehensively those who had portrayed the '98 rebellion as a series of disjointed, unconnected episodes. Instead he showed the United Irishmen as a cohesive, revolutionary, ideologically based society whose clear aim of a democratic secular republic had captured the imagination of great masses of the Irish people. He was concerned also to rebut the accusations about the Rising, particularly that Wexford was a Jacquerie largely motivated by sectarianism, or that there was not Protestant participation and leadership in that county.

The Fenians and the Catholic Church
competing for the memory of '98

The Fenians, more properly titled the Irish Republican Brotherhood, were a revolutionary oath-bound secret society that emerged in the late 1850s. Many had been Young Irelanders. The IRB organised in Ireland, America and Britain. Their aim was to 'break the connection with England', by force if necessary, and establish a republic. The Fenians/IRB believed that their secular Republicanism stood in direct relation to that of the United Irish patriots. They cited Miles Byrne's *Memoirs* as proof of this, and published extracts from them in their *Irish People* newspaper which began publication in 1863.[29] They began commemorating '98 when it was neither fashionable nor politically profitable, and while the Catholic Church remained opposed to the United Irish memory. The Fenians realised the potency of the memory of the martyred dead, and introduced graveside commemoration. Fenian treks to Bodenstown resulted in so much filching of souvenir chippings from Tone's gravestone that in the 1870s a locked railing had to be introduced for its preservation. Their commemorative obsequies lent legitimacy to the Fenian claim to be the latter-day bearers of the United Irish torch, passed down to them via Young Ireland.

The first monument to '98 was erected at St Mary's cemetery, Bunclody, Co. Wexford in 1875.[30] A year later, a Celtic cross was installed on French Hill outside Castlebar, Co. Mayo, to commemorate events there in 1798.[31] A further stone Celtic cross, by a sculptor from Enniscorthy, John Cullen, costing £120, was unveiled at Boolavogue on 29 September 1878 before a crowd of several hundred. Commissioned by the Fenian-dominated Dublin '98 Club, it bore carved crossed pikes and a dedication to Fr John Murphy. The parish priest of Ferns, Fr Bernard Meyler, described the '98 club as a den of 'communists and freemasons' and was hostile to the commemoration. The local parish priest, Fr Connick, objected to the pikes on the cross.[32] He refused to allow the IRB to erect the memorial to Fr Murphy on church property, and forbade parishioners from attending the unveiling. He enforced the closure of local pubs on the day. Ironically, by the year of the '98 centenary, clerical attitudes had changed to such an extent that the Boolavogue memorial was moved into the churchyard.

The priest's action at Boolavogue was in line with the Church's blanket condemnation of the IRB as a violent, oath-bound secret society. For Cardinal Paul Cullen, 'Hell was not hot enough, nor eternity long enough' for his Republican opponents. The Cardinal's condemnation extended to the rising of 1798, in which 'all our patriots were tinged with infidelity, the two Sheares, Emmet, etc.'.[33] Cullen's attitude to '98 was coloured by his experience in Rome of the radical opponents of the universal Church. Drawing parallels with Continental anti-clerical revolutionaries, such as Mazzini and Garibaldi, he dismissed the Fenians as 'Godless nobodies'.[34] Indeed, Irish Catholics were directly involved in shoring up the Papal States against the Italian radicals. Famously, an Irish brigade, fighting with the international volunteers, dubbed 'Papal Zouaves', defeated the Garibaldini in a hand-to-hand bayonet fight.

Fr Kavanagh, Faith and Fatherland

To avoid giving the Fenians a free hand in the commemoration of the United Irishmen and '98, which undoubtedly had mass appeal, the Catholic Church began to move from its position of complete opposition. Instead, it adapted and shaped the memory of '98 to conform more to the Catholic Nationalist model than the secular version of the Republicans.

The Church was engaged in a cold war with the IRB for the hearts and minds of Nationalist Ireland. It had a major weapon in the person of Fr Patrick Kavanagh, a Franciscan historian from Wexford. Kavanagh's *A Popular History of the Insurrection of 1798* (Dublin, 1870) posed a very different thesis to that of the Republicans. In Kavanagh's version, the 'morally pure' Catholic peasantry of Wexford, led by their heroic priests, only finally rose in defence of their homes and churches in the face of the utmost provocation of their sectarian tormentors. In this scenario, the Society of United Irishmen, and by implication Protestants, had no place: 'When Wexford stood at bay the United Irishmen were not to be found.'[35] For generations, Fr Kavanagh's 'Faith and Fatherland' version of '98, with nine further editions published up to 1928, would be the dominant mainstream Nationalist interpretation. It also fitted well with the ideology of constitutional Nationalism, particularly for many in the Irish Parliamentary Party who were opposed to the Fenian project of a secular republic on the lines posited by the United Irishmen and Young Ireland. They nevertheless felt impelled to pay lip-service to the United Irish memory, given its potency among even moderate Nationalists.

2

The 1898 Centenary

The Cave Hill Compact, Belfast 1795
The Shamrock, December 1890, J.D.F. Reigh

THE BATTLE WITHIN NATIONALISM over the legacy of the United Irishmen came to a head during the centenary commemorations. Constitutional Nationalism was divided to the point of impotence as a result of the demise of Parnell in 1891 and the failure of the Home Rule Bill of 1893. Many Nationalists, particularly the young, disillusioned with the political process, had turned to the 'New Nationalist' or 'Irish-Ireland' movements such as the Gaelic Athletic Association and the Gaelic League, which stressed culture, language and identity.

Loyalism, on the other hand, appeared to be in the ascendant. There was a solid Conservative and Unionist majority in the House of Commons, and the Government's 'Constructive Unionism', designed to mitigate the demand for Home Rule, appeared to be successful. 1897 was a particularly bad year for Nationalists as they had to witness the splendour of the celebrations in Ireland, north and south, of Queen Victoria's Diamond Jubilee. The heart of Unionist Dublin, in particular the area from College Green to St Stephen's Green, was bedecked with representations of the monarch, Union flags, and red, white and blue bunting.

Nationalists agreed that a counterpoise to the Jubilee was crucial, not least in order to restore their flagging self-respect and morale. The centenary of the United Irish Rising in 1898 clearly provided an opportunity. A National Commemoration Committee was set up early in 1897. This was primarily an IRB initiative, and its President was the veteran Fenian/Young Irelander, John O'Leary. The divided Parliamentary Party factions were at first tepid, but, witnessing the growing popular support, they eventually jumped onto the gathering centenary bandwagon. The competing traditions of revolutionary and constitutional Nationalism saw the centenary as an opportunity to reassert their influence and gain recruits. Many constitutionalists, weary of internecine strife, hoped to reunite the disparate strands of the Parliamentary Party.

The Fenian majority on the National Commemoration

Committee had good reason to fear a take-over by their parliamentary opponents, and sought to exclude MPs from the executive. In principle, the IRB and other radicals such as James Connolly, Maud Gonne and Alice Milligan felt strongly that the constitutionalists should be excluded on the grounds that they were opposed to the ideology, aims and methods of the United Irishmen.

The parliamentarians cried foul, and a good deal of time was wasted in wrangling over the composition of the committee, to the point of scandal. This jockeying for position was a hindrance to the effective organisation of the centenary commemoration. Indeed, John Dillon, leader of the majority parliamentary faction, at first set up his own rival Centenary Association. His rival, John Redmond – scion of an ancient Wexford family – claimed ancestors on both sides in '98. He wrote a pamphlet, *The Truth about '98*, in 1886, and the Rising had long been a recurrent theme in support of his position in the politics of his own day.

Eventually, in March 1898, a compromise was reached and places were allocated on the Commemoration Committee to representatives of the parliamentary factions led by Dillon and Redmond. In fact, the parliamentarians brought on board their internecine disputes, to the detriment of the commemorations. However, the Fenians and their fellow-travellers maintained overall direction of the national commemorative events, through their investment of enthusiasm, time and effort.[36]

The main thrust of the centenary would be the erection in the heart of Dublin, at the north-west corner of St Stephen's Green, of a monument to Wolfe Tone. Memorials were also planned all over the country, and local '98 clubs were set up for the purpose. At regional level, the constitutionalists were more in control by virtue of their local constituency organisations, the support of Nationalist newspapers and the Catholic clergy. There was a separate commemorative organisation in Britain, of which William Butler Yeats was Chairman.

The north in the centenary year

In Ulster, the organisation of commemoration was fragmented among different Nationalist groupings. Fifty-three '98 clubs in Ulster comprised some 11,000 paid-up members, including 19 clubs in Belfast with a membership of some 5,000. At a meeting of interested parties that he called in September 1897, the Dillonite Joe Devlin gained control of the Belfast '98 clubs. The poet Alice Milligan, with a few fellow Republican sympathisers, left the meeting in disgust. In Milligan's view, opportunistic parliamentarians who had no real sympathy with the aims or principles of the United Irishmen had hijacked the centenary commemorations in the city.[37] In addition, Devlin apparently was keen to run an independent Belfast operation, whereas Milligan was anxious to keep open links to the Central Committee in the capital:

> Miss Milligan claimed that they could accomplish union by standing by the '98 Executive … An exceedingly grave division at present existed among nationalists in Belfast, and the '98 movement should be guarded from being involved in it. Mr Devlin protested that this last remark was an insult to the Nationalists of Belfast and said Miss Milligan should not be heard. He objected to any man from Dublin coming down to interfere in Belfast.[38]

Milligan also wished to involve women in the '98 commemorations, which were male-dominated, and to this end founded the Irish Women's Centenary Union in October 1897.[39]

Elsewhere in Ulster, the '98 clubs were dominated by the Fenians, except in Derry and Tyrone, where the Irish National Foresters controlled them. A serious problem with commemoration in Ulster was that, due to its sectarian geography, '98 monuments could not be safely erected in many areas. Therefore most northern '98 clubs had to content themselves with the fabrication of ornate banners depicting United Irish figures and 1798 scenes or events. These were startlingly similar in design to those of the Orange lodges, as many of the Ulster '98 clubs employed the principal Orange banner-makers, such as Bridgetts of Belfast.

Ulster Protestant Nationalists
and the centenary

Protestant participation in the Ulster commemorations was confined to a small but effective minority of high-profile Nationalists, notably Alice Milligan and the antiquarian and Hibernicist, Francis Joseph Bigger. His house, Ard Righ on the Antrim Road in Belfast, was for many years a meeting place for leading lights in the Irish-Ireland movement and Nationalist activists. Bigger, a member of the Church of Ireland and a prominent solicitor and Freemason, revived the *Ulster Journal of Archaeology* in 1894, with the unearthing of material on '98 as a main aim. One contributor to this was Rev. W.S. Smith of Antrim, whose *Memories of '98* – a rather melodramatic account of the 'turn-out' gleaned from members of his congregation – was serialised. Copies of this are held in the Bigger Collection in Belfast Central Library. Bigger himself wrote and published *Remember Orr, the life of the United Irish Presbyterian martyr William Orr*.[40] It was the only one of Bigger's series of the *Lives of the United Irish Leaders of the North* to reach publication. The manuscripts of this series are also held in the Bigger Collection in Belfast Central Library.

Alice Milligan was of central importance in the centenary in Belfast and nationally. Milligan, a Methodist born in Omagh in 1866, was educated at Methodist College Belfast and settled in the city in 1888. Aware of the gap in her schooling in terms of Irish history, she read avidly, becoming a Nationalist in the process. With the zeal of the convert, Milligan bombarded both fellow Protestants and 'lukewarm' Catholics with Nationalist propaganda.[41] She was a founder member of the Henry Joy McCracken Literary Society in 1895, and edited its journal *The Northern Patriot*. Following its demise, she ran the Nationalist monthly *The Shan Van Vocht* with her Catholic colleague, Anna Johnston (a.k.a. Ethna Carbery). This appeared from January 1896 until its demise in early 1899, and was a vehicle for both Nationalist propaganda and Irish culture. The centenary commemorations took up many of its pages, which were awash with exhortations to revive the spirit of '98 and with ballads, stories, essays, and reports of visits to graves and battle-sites.

At the inaugural meeting in Dublin of the National Commemoration Committee, in March 1897, Milligan and Johnston were among the five representatives elected for Ulster. Incidentally, the Ulster pair, along with Maud Gonne, appear to have been the only female members of the Committee. As we shall see, the participation of Protestant Nationalists in the centenary commemorations was in stark contrast to the attitudes of the vast majority of their co-religionists.

Centenary events

The centenary commemorations kicked off on New Year's Eve 1897 with torchlight parades all over Nationalist Ireland, the largest being in Dublin, Belfast, Limerick and Cork. A commemorative group in Belfast climbed to McArt's Fort, the scene of the Cave Hill Compact of 1795, when Tone, McCracken, Simms and Neilson swore 'never to desist in our efforts, until we have subverted the authority of England over our country and asserted our independence'. At the summit, the party lit a dozen pitch-barrels and invoked the United Irish memory, before heading down to join the main Belfast parade on the Nationalist Falls Road. In some parts of Belfast and Ulster there was hostility and even attacks from Loyalists. In the following year there were many events throughout the country at which the 'spirit of '98' was invoked in the rhetoric of overheated orators. John O'Leary, Maud Gonne, John Redmond, John Dillon, Fr Kavanagh and Alice Milligan were much in demand as speakers. The two main events in the commemorative calendar were undoubtedly the grand parades in Belfast and Dublin in the summer.

Monday 6 June was the anniversary of the Battle of Antrim. The commemorative parade along Belfast's Falls Road, from Smithfield Square to Hannahstown Hill, was attended by many thousands of marchers and onlookers. The fact that the parade was confined to the Catholic heartland of the city graphically illustrated the geographical limitation of commemoration to the Nationalist areas. The Nationalist *Irish News*'s description of the previous day's march and meeting at Hannahstown is now quoted at length as it gives a

1798 – centenary procession on the Falls Road

ULSTER MUSEUM

clear indication of the militant spirit of even constitutional Nationalism as the centenary year progressed. The devotion of these mainly Catholic Nationalists of 1898 to the memory of the Presbyterian insurgents of '98 is also clear:

> In Smithfield the scene was a stirring one and but for the rain would have even been gay. The flags and banners of the clubs certainly presented an inspiring sight and the orderliness with which the processionists formed and the crowd behaved was very creditable ... The head of the Procession began to move at about half-past ten.
>
> The following bands took part: National Brass Band, St Patrick's, Lord Edward, Hearts of Down, National Flute Band, Sexton Flute Band, Grattan, St Peter's, Mandeville, Henry Joy McCracken Greencastle, Castlewellan (County Down), Dundrum (County Down), Downpatrick, Henry Joy McCracken Belfast, O'Connell, St Joseph's, Wolfe Tone, and Emmet Guards. Immense crowds lined the way all along, but no disturbance of any kind occurred until Dover Street was reached.

The paper then describes a number of Loyalist attacks on the parade, which were repulsed by the police:

> The remainder of the march was entirely without incident until the place of meeting was being neared. As Hannahstown Hill was being ascended a considerable crowd could be seen coming over the brow of Black Mountain, and they were not long in making known their hostile intentions waving in the air large bludgeons which they were carrying, and otherwise behaving in a threatening manner. Before the procession got to the top, luckily, a body of police went up and succeeded in putting these gentlemen to the rout. The march to the ground was not afterwards interfered with.

The meeting

> The meeting was addressed from one platform, on which were – Mrs M.T. Pender[42] and Miss Pender, Messrs John Dillon M.P.; Michael McCartan M.P.; Jeremiah Jordan, a Methodist M.P., Joseph Devlin, J.T. Donovan, W.D. Harbinson, W. Robinson, T. Agnew, John Clarke, H. Byrne and Miss Watson, hon. secs Belfast and Ulster United Centenary Association ... the chair was taken by Mr Joseph Devlin, President of the Belfast and Ulster United Centenary Association. In opening the proceedings, he said they were assembled that day on that historic ground to commemorate the rebellion of 100 years ago [cheers] when their Protestant and Presbyterian forefathers fought and died for Ireland. [cheers] ... A century had passed away since British brutality had murdered Henry Joy McCracken and the spirit which animated the men of that day still lived amongst them. They were rebels in Heart, and they would be rebels in reality if they had the chance [cheers] rebels in so far as they believed that those sentiments of Nationality would never be eradicated from the hearts of Belfast Nationalists until every vestige of British rule in Ireland was rooted out of the country from one end to the other. [cheers] Some people said that they should let those old memories die and that they were not persecuted now as they were in 1798, but while the weapons of British rule in Ireland at present were not the pitch cap and the bayonet, they still carried on a more refined system of torture in starving hundreds and thousands of their countrymen in the South and West of Ireland, and impudent British statesman sneered at the

poverty of their people – poverty which was brought about by years and centuries of British rule …

On the platform that day they had the Leader of the Irish Party, Mr John Dillon [cheers] who led the constitutional party so long as constitutionalism would play the Irish game, but who would be a rebel tomorrow, as his father had been in 1848. [cheers] … During the past twelve months they had formed one splendid organisation of '98 clubs, the strength and power of which was exemplified in that glorious meeting. Let those '98 clubs live, and continue to exercise that splendid influence on the body politic which they had exercised with such good results as to bring men and women of all sections of politics within the National move-ment on one common National platform. [loud cheers] They hailed that day – the centenary of the battle of Antrim – as a glo-rious day for the future of the National movement. He rejoiced that they had turned out in such large numbers to honour the memories of the men of '98. [cheers]

Mr John Dillon M.P., who was received with prolonged cheer-ing, said – I am proud of Belfast and proud of Ulster today, for … I have never seen a more imposing demonstration than you have made here today in the … capital of Ulster [cheers] to celebrate the principles and to commemorate the men of '98, and to announce to the world that you are faithful to these principles, and you revere the memory of these men … here in Ulster, aye, in Belfast itself, the spirit of the United Irishmen is alive today as it was when Wolfe Tone founded that great association here in this city 100 years ago … Now the question has often been asked why we cele-brate the memories of '98 and men have been asked why we recall those bitter memories and stir them up again … Because we are a nation, and because we are proud of the men who in dark and evil days staked their lives and all they had on earth for the National rights of Ireland. And there never was a nation of men worthy of a place amongst the nations of the earth who did not rejoice to cel-ebrate the anniversaries of any gallant deeds which were done in the course of their National history … and on the day on which … Ireland would forget Wolfe Tone and the United Irishmen her name should be blotted from amongst the nations of the earth. We celebrate their memory, because after 100 years we believe in their principles and we celebrate their deeds, because they fought not only for the liberty of Ireland but for human liberty, and the prin-

ciples which they defended with their blood have been the principles of every free people from the day of the United Irishmen down
to this hour ... In the year 1791, on the 14th October, in the city
in which you live, was founded by Wolfe Tone the first club of the
United Irish Society ... the men who founded the United Irish
Society were not Catholics – the United Irish Society was founded
... by Protestant merchants of Belfast. But they were honourable
men, far different from many of their successors today ... And
although this society was founded ... by ... Protestants, that did
not prevent the Catholic people of Ireland rallying round them,
and within three years this association ... counted within its ranks
upwards of 300,000 of the Catholic men, and shoulder to shoulder and arm to arm they marched on in that great struggle for
human freedom and although they failed ... all that has come to
Ireland from that day to now in the way of emancipation and
reform, and the freedom of the people, is in my opinion the direct
continuation of the work and the fruit of the sacrifices of the
United Irishmen of '98.[43]

Although apologies were read from John Redmond MP and other
Nationalist politicians of various hues, this was clearly a Dillonite
occasion. The leader of that faction of the divided Irish Party was
the principal invited speaker, heralded by his main lieutenant in the
north Joe Devlin. Devlin, 'the coming man', not yet MP for West
Belfast, was obviously using his control over the '98 clubs in Belfast
and the commemorative events as a vehicle for his advancement.

The parade made its way back to Smithfield largely without further attention from opponents. The banners of '98 clubs carried on
that occasion were afterwards carefully wrapped and stored. Some
would be used again during the '98 commemoration march along
the same road in 1948. However, the ramifications of the parade
and the hostility it provoked in Loyalist areas were to continue after
it had ended. That night there was extensive rioting, with looting
and house-wrecking in the city centre and in Protestant working-
class areas. This was especially intense in the Shankill district, where
there were sustained ferocious attacks on police. Indeed, the police
were on the verge of being overwhelmed when the Inniskilling
Dragoons were called in and, with lances at the ready, they finally
succeeded in sweeping the rioters off the streets.[44]

Loyalist hostility
to the centenary

Sectarianism had gained ground during the nineteenth century. Belfast, the old liberal town known as 'the Athens of the North' and virtual capital of the United Irishmen at the end of the eighteenth century, had greatly expanded due to the industrial revolution. Now known as 'Linenopolis', it was heading towards city status at the end of the nineteenth century. It attracted torrents of incoming workers from surrounding counties such as Armagh, many of whom brought with them the rabidly sectarian attitudes of their former homes.

As we have seen, the ultramontane tendency was supreme in Rome and throughout the Catholic world, not least in Ireland. The underlying sectarian bad feeling continued to manifest in the disputes over the Mater Hospital set up by the Sisters of Mercy in Belfast and the Catholic University question in Dublin. Unionist antipathy to the developments within Nationalism culminated in resistance to attempts by Gladstone's Liberal Government to introduce Home Rule in 1886 and 1893. Gladstone greatly misread the feelings of Irish Presbyterians, many of whom had been his supporters, in his desire to get their acquiescence to Home Rule. This was apparent in his appeal that they 'retain and maintain the tradition of their United Irish sires'.[45]

The politico-religious underpinnings of Unionism dovetailed in the slogan 'Home Rule is Rome Rule'. Since the Act of Union, Presbyterians and other Protestants had closed ranks politically and theologically. Presbyterian United Irishmen were believed by their descendants to have been, at best, simply fighting for political and religious equality or tenant rights. Those who were undeniably Republican separatists were depicted either as misguided or as traitors who had acted against the best interests of their own community. Furthermore, both liberty and prosperity would be lost if Ireland was placed under a Home Rule parliament. This undoubtedly would be dominated by Roman Catholics inimical to Protestantism, and agriculturalists who were unsympathetic or hostile to the industrial prosperity of the north-east.

For most Presbyterians, circumstances had vastly changed since the time of the United Irishmen. Much of what they had sought since the Act of Union had been achieved. The Presbyterian lawyer J.J. Shaw, a former Professor at Magee College, Derry, argued that:

> Catholic Emancipation, a reformed parliament, a responsible executive and equal laws for the whole Irish people. These were the real and declared objects of the United Irishmen. And it was only because they saw no hope of attaining these objects through an Irish parliament that they took up arms.[46]

Now that this settlement was under threat from the Liberal Government of Gladstone, his erstwhile supporters turned against him with the vitriol of the spurned. This attitude was most cogently expressed by a Liberal businessman, Thomas Sinclair, at an anti-Home Rule rally in 1886, with a backward glance at the Presbyterians who had turned out in 1798:

> Would it be a triumph of civilisation if, after having, by eighty-six years of gradual justice, transfigured the Ulster rebels of '98 into the most loyal and devoted subjects of the realm, she [England] were now, by a grand act of injustice, to turn back the shadow on the dial and invite the return of hours of darkness and despair?[47]

The attacks on the June 1898 parade in Belfast were symptomatic of a general Protestant hostility to the Nationalist-organised '98 commemorations. The 1798 Rising in Ulster had been mainly a Presbyterian affair. Ironically, in 1898 it was being commemorated primarily by Catholics, in areas with little or no connection with the events of 1798.

Presbyterians in the north were now to a great extent loyal, and hostile to the commemoration of the exploits of many of their ancestors. Loyalists therefore excluded themselves from the centenary events except to repel intruders coming into their areas with the intention of commemoration. For instance, by June 1898 there was only one '98 club in Down, a county where the United Irishmen had been out in great numbers.

The events of the centenary year reinforced Unionist determination not to make any concessions to Nationalists, who apparently gloried in the efficacy of armed insurrection. Unionist hostility to the 1898 commemorations simply underlined their feelings of separateness. The dominant thinking in Loyalist circles was that there were two nations in Ireland. Loyalists were increasingly alienated from the rest of Ireland by the growth of Irish-Ireland movements such as the GAA and the Gaelic League. This position was entrenched by Loyalist pride in the industrial growth of the northeast, which they contrasted favourably with the agrarian economy of the south and west.

Apart from the attacks on the Belfast '98 parade in June, northern Loyalist hostility to the '98 celebrations was mainly confined to the columns of Unionist newspapers. The Grand Master of the Grand Lodge of Belfast, Rev. Dr R.R. Kane, wrote in connection with the June commemorations in the city to the Unionist *Belfast Evening Telegraph*:

> Will you allow me to commend to the thoughtful attention of the loyalist public of Belfast the resolutions herewith sent to you and passed this night at the monthly meeting of the Grand Orange Lodge of Belfast. I would further ask loyal men to remember that if any serious disturbances were to arise in the city the loss (and it would be very great) would not fall upon the rebel processionists, who have absolutely no stake in the city, but upon the loyalist population. Further, it would seriously interfere with the good feeling and mutual confidence and respect so rapidly growing up between the protestant people of our city and province and the more respectable Roman Catholic people whose many amiable qualities we all so thoroughly appreciate. I earnestly trust the loyal men and women of our city will attend with double diligence to their business on Monday, June 6, and reserve themselves for the coming July celebration which we expect will be of unusual interest and magnitude.

The following is the official communication referred to in the above letter.

> In reply to a communication addressed to the Grand Lodge of Belfast, requesting the Grand Lodge to assist in organising a counter-demonstration to the demonstration to be held in Belfast on June 6 in commemoration and in honour of the Rebellion of 1798,

the following resolutions were unanimously passed at the monthly meeting of the Grand Lodge, held on the evening of June 1 in the Orange Hall, Clifton Street.

(Signed) R.R. Kane, Grand Master;
Thomas Johnston, Grand Sec.

That it would be entirely contrary to the principles of the Loyal Orange Institution to interfere with any section of our fellow-citizens in celebrating whatever event in their history commends itself to their good taste and deliberate judgement as deserving of public commemoration and honour.

That while we regard the proposed demonstration of June 6 as a flatigious display of sympathy with an armed insurrection, and, which, above all things, was characterised by a series of most foul and cowardly murders and massacres of innocent men and women whose only offence was their Protestantism, we fully recognise that it is for the constituted authorities, and for them only, to say whether such demonstration is to be allowed or prohibited.

That we feel quite confident that the Orangemen of this city will, in accordance with their principles and obligations, abstain from all attempts to molest the demonstration, and we most earnestly advise all other Protestants to remember that the very genius of Protestantism is to allow to all others as full a liberty as we claim for ourselves. We further remind our friends that any attempt to molest the demonstration on their part would bring them into a position in which Protestants and Loyalists should never be found – a position of hostility to those who are commissioned by her Majesty the Queen to administer the law, and to maintain peace, order and liberty amongst her Majesty's Subjects.

Richard R. Kane, LLD GM[48]
Thos Johnston GS

God save the Queen.[49]

The *Belfast Evening Telegraph* covered the 6 June parade in Belfast and vividly depicted the reasons for Loyalist hostility to the commemorations, opening with the mocking headline:

Damp Weather – Damp Demonstrators – Damp Speeches

It will not be out of place to briefly sketch the object with which the display has been organised. To those acquainted with the history of Ireland, the information conveyed will of course be familiar, but there are many – and principally amongst those who talk most loudly about the glories of Ninety-eight, who have scarcely the faintest conception of the aims and motives of the rebels of one-hundred years ago, or the means by which they attempted to break the link which then bound this country to the other isle. The original body which promoted the rising was that known as the United Irishmen and its most prominent leaders were drawn from the North of Ireland, notably Down and Antrim, Belfast being the centre where they met. Throughout Ireland they found numerous adherents, and it is a remarkable fact that in the counties of Wexford and Wicklow they obtained little or no support. There the rebels were led by priests, who had scarcely any connection with the United Irishmen's movement – which was Republican and socialistic in its tendency – with the result that the rebellion in those counties was characterised throughout with the most brutal atrocities which have ever disgraced the history of a country. Those atrocities were perpetrated upon the Protestant minority and in those counties still the holocaust of Scullabogue and the brutalities of Wexford are still remembered with horror by the descendants of those who were the victims of a fury as degrading as it was inhuman. The Wexford rebellion was brought to an end by the battle of Vinegar Hill towards the end of May …[50]

This analysis is remarkably similar to that of Fr Kavanagh, though from a different political standpoint. The paper goes on to state that the battles of Antrim and Ballynahinch, which took place in June, had no real connection with the insurrection in Wexford:

The descendants of the men who rose in those days are now amongst the most loyal in the British Empire, and the parties who today assembled in Smithfield Square were neither their political nor family descendants. The United Irishmen of Antrim and Down were mainly Presbyterian. They fought honourably, unlike the rebels of the south and took their beating with good grace. The

men who today assembled can scarcely be said to have the slightest
right to commemorate their deeds. Those of Wexford are more in
their line.[51]

In staunchly Loyalist Sandy Row, Belfast, during the July 1898
'Twelfth' commemorations of the Battle of the Boyne, an Orange
Arch bore the legend 'Scullabogue Barn is ever green'. This was
commemoration of the other side of 1798. As such it was rare
indeed.

The grave of Betsy Gray

The destruction of the Betsy Gray gravestone near Ballynahinch
graphically illustrated the extent of Loyalist hostility in the north.
Betsy Gray, a Co. Down Presbyterian apparently slaughtered with
her brother and lover while fleeing the battlefield at Ballynahinch,
was a heroic figure to Nationalists in 1898. The hagiographical
Betsy Gray, or *Hearts of Down* by W.J. Lyttle, a Liberal newspaper
editor, published in 1888 was very popular, particularly in Co.
Down. Nevertheless, to most northern Loyalists she represented the
misguided, or indeed traitorous, past of sections of their community and something to be exorcised rather than commemorated.
Lyttle, at the time of publication, suggested the erection of a suitable monument to his heroine. However, it wasn't until 1896 that
one was finally erected, at Ballycreen, outside Ballynahinch, by a
man who claimed to be Betsy Gray's great-nephew.

Nationalist excursions to decorate the graves of martyrs and lay
wreaths at hallowed '98 spots had evoked from their opponents the
sneering epithet 'Charabanc Nationalists'. The announcement that
Nationalists were to hold a commemoration at the grave of Betsy
Gray on Sunday, 1 May 1898, was a provocation in this staunchly
Loyalist area that wasn't to be resisted. An affray resulted, after
which the monument was destroyed. This incident was widely and
variously reported in Nationalist and Unionist newspapers, each
side citing it to vilify the other.

The speech of Rev. L.A. Pooler at the 1898 'Twelfth' commemorations in Ballynahinch, soon after the incident at nearby
Ballycreen, is a good illustration of the change in Presbyterian

attitudes since 1798. His thesis was that the main demands of the United Irishmen had been met since the Act of Union:

> The United Men in the North, carried away with glowing accounts from their friends in America, and intoxicated by the excitement caused by the French revolution, dreamed of a great Republic. Out of every evil, however, God brought some good ... the rebellion furnished Lord Castlereagh and other statesmen with overwhelming arguments in favour of the Union, which took place two years afterwards ... He was happy to say that every constitutional reform which the Volunteers desired, and every grievance of which the United Men complained, had found a remedy long ago by a Parliament of the United Kingdom ... If an inhabitant of Ballynahinch in 1798 could stand there that day he would see great changes. He could see signs of industry and prosperity all around; he could see the descendants of the United Men in thousands praising God for the Union, and wearing Orange sashes; and he could see many a brave girl who would do a noble deed for her brother or a sweetheart as the heroine Betsy Gray.[52]

Romancing the stone

A third Belfast centenary commemorative parade, along the Falls Road, took place on 10 August. This was the procession accompanying the foundation stone destined for the proposed Dublin Wolfe Tone monument, to its place of dedication at Waterford Street on the Falls Road. The stone was hewn at McArt's Fort, the site of the 1795 Cave Hill Compact, and therefore of the utmost symbolic importance. For reasons of security it was impossible to have a United Irish monument in Belfast, but this was the next best thing, while at the same time providing a symbiotic link with the site in the capital. The *Irish News* reported the colourful scene:

> Last night the clubs of the city assembled on the Falls Road to take part in the ceremony of unveiling which was performed by Mr P.A. McHugh M.P., Mayor of Sligo. The following clubs, amongst others, were represented – the Neilson, Russell, Dr Drennan, Wm. Orr, West Belfast, McCracken, St Malachy's, and Mat McLenaghan [sic – McClenaghan]. The Mayor of Sligo, Mr Michael MacCartan, M.P. and others drove in a brake, shortly

before eight o'clock, from the Linenhall Hotel to Divis Street, where an enormous crowd had assembled. A procession was formed consisting of the several clubs, while the splendid banners with which they are equipped were carried. The St Paul's district occupied the van and preceding the foundation stone were the members of parliament and others. The lorry on which the stone was borne was handsomely decorated, as indeed were the animals which drew the interesting burden, while placed in front of the vehicle was the splendid banner of the Mary McCracken Club … Mr Joseph Devlin occupied the chair … Mr P.A. McHugh, Mayor, then formally unveiled the foundation stone, which bears the following inscription – 'A tribute from the Nationalists of Belfast, presented to the Belfast and Ulster United Centenary Association by P. Flanigan, Wolfe Tone 1798–1898.[53]

Wolfe Tone Day

When the stone arrived in Dublin, it lay in state for two nights in the old Newgate Gaol, with all its melancholy associations with the United Irishmen. The *Irish News* editorial, on 'Wolfe Tone Day', cogently put the Dublin parade in its historical context as an indication of the progress made by the Nationalist project since the 1798 Rising:

> Our people have reason … to congratulate themselves on the immense strides towards progress and larger freedom that have marked the intervening hundred years. Three score years ago a nationalist open-air parade and the laying of a national monument would have been proclaimed by Dublin Castle and prevented by horse, foot and artillery. Today the Government will look passively on accepting the inevitable with as good a grace as possible. All the best elements of Irish municipal and local life will be represented. Not many years ago those elements had no existence. Thirdly, Irishmen can rejoice at the assertion of Irish National spirit on a proud and grand scale. The spirit of the race is indestructible. It will never acquiesce in the rule of the stranger's serfdom which in every form is repugnant to it. National legislative independence alone will satisfy the nation's longings.[54]

One major disappointment for Nationalists was the fact that a much-heralded Irish-American participation failed to materialise. Although the '98 Centennial Association of America had made preparations for a massive pilgrimage, the Spanish–American War intervened. It wasn't only the presence of the exiles that was missed, but the tourist dollars they would have brought with them.[55]

The date chosen was 'Lady Day', 15 August, a feast-day laden with Catholic association, and now by popular ascription 'Wolfe Tone Day'. Naturally, there was criticism of the choice of this date. According to James Connolly, in the first ever issue of his *Workers' Republic* which was distributed at the demonstration, this date would be 'if not absolutely prohibitive to, at least bound to raise grave suspicion in the minds of our non-Catholic fellow-country-men'.[56]

The foundation stone was placed on a carriage and processed with great solemnity. It was flanked by an ornately costumed Irish National Forester guard of honour, followed by a huge throng with many bands and banners. It was the greatest event ever held to commemorate revolutionary Nationalism in Dublin. There were many contingents from the north, among which pride of place was given to a girl, dressed in green and gold, portraying Betsy Gray, the legendary heroine of the Battle of Ballynahinch. The onlookers reserved special cheers for the well-turned-out northerners.

The parade followed a three-mile route, touching on places associated with Tone and Emmet. It was three hours before it reached its designated site at St Stephen's Green. As a result of this conscious assertion of territorial imperative, this site would become a future place of assembly for Nationalist parades and demonstrations. John O'Leary, flanked by Irish Party leaders Dillon and Redmond, presided at the very moving and symbolically orchestrated stone-laying ceremony. This show of unity was somewhat soured by the refusal of Maud Gonne to share the platform with the constitutionalist politicians. O'Leary pronounced himself a living connection with 1867, 1848 and, by implication, 1798. He was presented with an ornate trowel, sent from America by Tone's grand-daughter, Mrs Charles Grace Maxwell, which had been touched by as many of the martyr's descendants as possible. O'Leary tapped the stone six times, to represent in turn each of Ireland's four provinces,

America and France. In conclusion, the band struck up the by now well-known 'Memory of the Dead', virtually the national anthem of Nationalism in 1898.[57]

The stone-laying ceremony was indeed the high point of the centenary commemorations. However, trains carrying northern participants back from the Dublin centenary celebrations in August were stoned and their occupants, having alighted, were molested by a mob outside the station in Belfast. Rioting extended into the city centre and shop windows were broken in Wellington Place.[58] Describing the commemorations as 'the '98 microbe', the *Belfast Evening Telegraph* stated that the speeches made by Nationalist parliamentarians at the Dublin commemoration on 15 August exposed their true nature: 'the mask has been thrown aside … patriots stood forth as openly-avowed rebels'.[59]

There was to be an anticlimactic denouement to the Wolfe Tone monument project. By the end of the centenary year, the politicians had lost interest in the monument, leaving it to the IRB and their associates. They, through a mixture of incompetence and corruption, failed to see the project through to completion. Only £561 of the necessary £14,000 had been raised by the end of 1898, most of which was in fact raised by the redoubtable Maud Gonne.[60] Worse still, most of that was embezzled. Eventually the lassitude of the commemorationists led to the galling usurpation of the site, which was requisitioned by the Corporation for the Dublin Fusilier Boer War memorial. Completed in 1911, this was to become known to Republicans as 'Traitors' Arch'. It is tempting to interpret this as a metaphor for the failure of Nationalism to best Unionism up to that point.[61]

Local monuments in 1898
and after

In many local areas the lasting centennial commemorative act was the erection of a permanent memorial to the martyrs of 1798. Close to 40 such memorials were erected. There was a keen sense of a national deficiency in patriotic monuments compared to other countries, and in particular given the extent of those erected to the

Loyalist cause throughout Ireland. This view was given rather force-ful expression by the Nationalist MP Sir Thomas Esmonde at the stone-laying ceremony in Wexford Town:

> while there are monuments in plenty to the alien representatives of English misrule in Ireland, the monuments commemorative of great Irishmen, of great events in Irish history, are few and far between. Our towns are studded with memorials of English kings, of English Lords Lieutenant ...[62]

These '98 monuments gave concrete expression to the growing sense of a separate national identity that was also embodied in Irish-Ireland movements such as the Gaelic League, the Irish literary revival and the Gaelic Athletic Association. Most of the statuary of 1898 and succeeding years, particularly the work of Ireland's leading monumental sculptor, the northern Protestant Oliver Sheppard, was highly influenced by the Fr Kavanagh interpretation of the Rising. Thus many of the figures on the monuments, espe-cially in Co. Wexford, were representations of heroic peasantry in working clothes rather than of United Irishmen in uniform. Sheppard's Enniscorthy monument shows a flag-draped Fr Murphy pointing the way to a young peasant insurgent. In many monu-ments the clear association is made also with the Catholic religion, with some adorned with rosary beads or crucifixes. In others there are female figures representing Ireland and/or 'Mary of the Gael'.[63] In Wexford there was virulent popular rejection of the Redmond proposal of a round tower monument on Vinegar Hill. It smacked too much of the constitutionalism of O'Connell, whose burial-place in Glasnevin was adorned with just such a round tower.

The siting of '98 monuments had historical/political significance. 1898 was also the year in which the Local Government Act hand-ed control to mostly Nationalist-dominated local councils. Now Nationalist monuments could be sited in prominent positions, such as town centres, from which Loyalist-controlled authorities such as the Grand Juries would previously have barred them. Nevertheless, this was a transitional period and in some areas a number of mon-uments still had to be sited on the periphery. Particularly galling to Nationalists was Lord Portsmouth's refusal to allow a monument to be erected on his property at Vinegar Hill. Due to factors of time and expense, several years would elapse before some monuments would finally be in place, in some cases as late as 1908. By that time they had become unfashionable in some quarters, particularly with constitutionalists wishing to project a less militant image for Nationalism. Many of the centenary monuments were simply not very good art. This was forcefully given expression by, among others, W.B. Yeats. Maud Gonne confessed to agreeing with Yeats, even though she was heavily involved in stone-laying and unveiling ceremonies because she recognised their educational and propaganda value.[64]

Merchandising '98

Low art also appeared during the centenary year as commemorative merchandise made its appeal to popular taste. Undoubtedly much of this was pure kitsch. For instance, the Belfast jewellers Wightman & Co. advertised, in the *Shan Van Vocht*, jewellery made from the chips left over from the cutting of the Wolfe Tone foundation stone. These were polished and incorporated into shamrock-shaped scarf-pins, harp-shaped brooches and Celtic Cross pendants. There were centenary bicycles, and a huge range of decorated handkerchiefs and ceramics. Leonard's Chemists in Dublin sold '98 Centenary perfume. Bushmills Whiskey, with its distillery sited in a staunchly Protestant village in Co. Antrim, proclaimed in advertisements that 'True Patriots drank Bushmills'. Posters, postcards and novels mostly portrayed the Faith and Fatherland/heroic priest-led peasantry version of '98. Huge numbers of copies of sheet-music ballads about '98 were sold. Those written at the time of the centenary eclipsed in popularity existing songs contemporary with the Rising. The most popular, such as Robert Dwyer Joyce's 'Boys of Wexford' and P.J. McCall's 'Boolavogue', followed the Kavanagh interpretation of events in 1798. The latter was properly titled 'Father Murphy of the County Wexford' and is sung to the older tune 'Youghal Harbour'. It first appeared in the *Irish Weekly Independent*, 18 June 1898. The first verse is a veritable synopsis of the Kavanagh thesis:

> At Boolavogue, as the sun was setting
> O'er the green May meadows of Shelmalier,
> A rebel hand set the heather blazing,
> And brought the neighbours from far and near,
> Then Father Murphy from old Kilcormack,
> Spurred up the rocks with a warning cry
> 'Arm! Arm!' he cried, 'for I've come to lead you
> Now priest and people must fight or die!'

The last verse invokes the past in a call to arms in the present.

> God give you glory, brave Father Murphy,
> And open heaven to all your men;
> The cause that called you may call tomorrow
> In another war for the Green again.

The popular Nationalist monthly periodicals and national weekly newspapers, such as the *The Shamrock*, *The Irish Emerald*, *The Weekly Freeman* and *United Ireland*, published high-quality cartoons portraying 1798 and other Nationalist historical themes. They are clearly Nationalist propaganda. These cartoons, principally by J.F. O'Hea, J.D. Reigh, Walter C. Mills, Thomas Fitzpatrick and Phil Blake, also filled a vacuum in the school curriculum which, largely for political reasons, contained little or no Irish history.[65] From a Nationalist perspective, this gap was also filled by the histories of A.M. Sullivan,[66] the novels of Charles Kickham and plays by, among others, Dion Boucicault and Yeats, notably the latter's celebrated *Cathleen Ni Houlihan*.

The political impact
of the centenary

In assessing the long-term and short-term impact of the centenary, a number of major points come to the fore. Firstly, the 1898 commemorations, which had kicked off with divisions among Nationalists, ended with the reopening of channels between the various constitutionalist factions. These led to the reunification of the Parliamentary Party in 1900, under John Redmond. However, a significant constitutionalist faction, led by William O'Brien, remained aloof from this détente. Also, as a result of the wave of United Irish sentiment during the commemorative year, a new generation of recruits came into the IRB, which for many stood in direct succession to the men of '98. The new blood gave the organisation renewed vigour. This cohort was later augmented by a further generation of IRB recruits which included Patrick Pearse and Sean MacDermott. Pearse in particular was influenced by '98. This grouping would provide the impetus for the next phase of separatist violence in the Easter Rising of 1916.

The Dublin Castle authorities, of course, were very interested in the impact of the centenary commemorations. The police reports provide a useful assessment in this respect. In his monthly report for February 1898, the Inspector General, RIC, Neville Chamberlain, noted that efforts to create popular enthusiasm for the centenary had:

> as yet met with very limited success. In very few localities indeed is there any enthusiasm exhibited; and where the movement has started with some show of popular favour dissension and disunion dogs its career.[67]

In December 1898, police reports still noted that 'the end of the Centenary year finds little result from the agitation beyond the erection of a few memorials'.[68] However, the Inspector General's report for October 1900 was much less sanguine, and referred to:

> the very serious wave of sedition which has spread over the country, and which found expression openly in many cases in election speeches last month. This seditious feeling was originally inflamed by the '98 demonstrations two years ago; which though they had no practical result at the time, undoubtedly revived the old feeling of animosity to England, and awakened anew the sentiment of Irish independent nationality.[69]

Interesting back-up to this last view is provided by the song 'John MacBride's Brigade'.[70] It is about the Irish volunteers, under the command of Maud Gonne's husband, Major John MacBride, who fought on the side of the Boers against the British in South Africa.

In the second verse of three, the Irish volunteers wreak vengeance for '98:

> Three thousand Transvaal Irishmen, with spirits brave and free,
> They struck the Saxon foemen down at Glencoe and Dundee.
> From Ladysmith and Spion Kop their flag victorious waved,
> And well they wreaked revenge on those who Erin's Isle enslaved.
> With guns and bayonets in their hands, their Irish flag on high,
> As down they swept on England's ranks out rang their battle cry
> 'Revenge! Remember '98, and how our fathers died.'
> 'We'll pay the English back today', cried fearless John MacBride.

3

'98 Commemoration
in the Twentieth Century

1948 Belfast parade led by the Irish Transport and
General Workers' Union Band, enters Corrigan Park

A S WE HAVE SEEN, the work of the National Commemoration Committee of 1898 had tailed off in a welter of recrimination and apathy. As a result of the ultimate failure to erect the monument to Wolfe Tone in Dublin, the focus in the 1900s switched to his grave at Bodenstown, where there had been annual IRB commemorations on Tone's birthday, 20 June, since 1891. 'Also, the spotlight of commemoration now shone on that other romantic nationalist icon Robert Emmet. Just as his rebellion in 1803 might by described as a postscript to '98, 1903 provided an echo of the commemorative events of 1898, culminating on 20 September, the exact centenary of Emmet's execution, with a march in Dublin attended by some 80,000.'

Patrick Pearse, one of the new IRB generation, illustrated the efficacy of commemoration as propaganda, particularly at the graveside. At a massive IRB commemoration in Bodenstown in 1913, Pearse described Tone as 'the greatest of Irish Nationalists'. In graveside orations at the funerals of the Fenians, John O'Leary in 1913 and O'Donovan Rossa in 1915, Pearse's invocations of the 'patriot dead' began with Tone and the United Irishmen. Commemoration now served as a major vehicle of Republican propaganda and recruitment.

Something of a hiatus in commemoration followed the death of Pearse and his IRB comrades in 1916. Republicans were heavily involved in desperate struggles of their own, in the process creating a new generation of martyrs for future commemoration. After Partition and the bitterness engendered by the Civil War, the Free State authorities had neither the inclination nor the resources to put commemoration or the upkeep of monuments on their list of priorities. They wanted rather to cool the heat generated by such commemoration as they strove with difficulty to establish control over the new state.

By the mid-1920s, following a period of despair and disillusionment arising out of their defeat in the Civil War, Republicans were beginning to regroup. In line with this revival was a reignited enthusiasm for the commemoration of national martyrs. As a result, in 1926, the National Graves Association (NGA) was constituted as a permanent body to oversee the upkeep of patriot graves and monuments. '98 memorials in the care of the NGA include Wolfe Tone's grave at Bodenstown, monuments to Bartholomew Teeling at Collooney, Co. Sligo, Roddy McCorley, Toomebridge, Co. Antrim and The Croppy Boy/Pikeman in Tralee, Co. Kerry. National bodies such as the Irish National Foresters, Ancient Order of Hibernians and Gaelic Athletic Association kept the memory of the United Irishmen alive in the names of branches and on their banners.

The erection of '98 monuments continued in a desultory manner during the 1930s and early 1940s. Accounts of dedication speeches show that, as well as referring to the '98 era, they generally reflected the politics of their time. An instance of this occurred at Ballinamuck during the dedication of the '98 monument, on 9 September 1928, the 120th anniversary of the battle. Executed in Sicilian marble by Farrells of Glasnevin, the monument presents a wounded pikeman, with broken pike-shaft, backing onto a tree. The newspaper account of the event gives some interesting insights into the state of politics and attitudes to '98 at the time. The platform chairman was Canon John Keville, Parish Priest, Drumlish. Among those on the platform were Lord and Lady Longford and a number of TDs (members of the Irish parliament) from Government and Opposition. Small wonder that Canon Keville expressed the hope:

> That as chairman my duties will be light and that good order and decency will prevail at the meeting and that there will be no interruptions and no questions asked, that each speaker will get a respectful hearing.[71]

Lord Longford spoke first in Irish. Although an ancestor had been a British army officer at the Battle of Ballinamuck in 1798, he was sympathetic to the actions and ideals of the United Irishmen and their French allies:

> The soldiers of France had fought before in the cause of liberty

when led by Joan of Arc, recently sainted. France was set free from
the tyranny of English monarchy and English government ... In
honouring the memory of those who died, let us take a lesson from
their sacrifice. They were not afraid to give up all for their country
and it is for us to use every effort to make it a great nation. Dia
Saor Éire [sic].[72]

Canon Keville, who had earlier spoken in praise of the Free State,
was drawn into an altercation with J.J. Killane TD (Fianna Fáil),
who stated that:

It is futile for us to come here if we do not renew our faith. There
is hardly any one of us who does not feel pride in honouring the
hallowed spot where some ancestor fell. Let us not come here to
honour a beautiful work of art – a beautiful milestone. No let us
renew our Republican pledge that ...

This obviously made the Canon see red and he told Mr Killane to
sit down, which he did immediately. However, his Fianna Fáil colleague, M.J. Kennedy TD, complained that the clergy were always
keen to ban the word 'Republican' – even when commemorating
the greatest Republicans in Irish history.[73]

Bodenstown

Bodenstown continued to be the main focus of Republican and
Nationalist commemoration of the United Irishmen. Upon the
establishment of the Free State, and thereafter, it assumed an official aspect and visits by the leading politicians of the new state
became *de rigueur*. These kept well away from the pilgrimages of
the revolutionaries and radicals. As a result, and also due to ensuing
divisions and splits in Republicanism down the years, there has
been a multiplicity of commemorative parades to Bodenstown
churchyard each year.

   In the 1930s the various tributes at Bodenstown reflected the het-
erogeneous nature of Republicanism at the time. As well as the IRA,
Communists and members of the left-leaning Republican Congress
attended parades numbered in the thousands. In 1934, Protestants
from the Shankill and east Belfast marched in the ranks of the

Republican Congress. This was a spin-off from the Outdoor Relief protests of 1932. In that year, for a brief moment, vast numbers of unemployed from Protestant and Catholic working-class Belfast had cast aside their ancient sectarian hatreds to force the Government to reform the iniquitous Poor Law system, which had been overwhelmed in the Depression. Amazingly, the Belfast group became involved in a fracas with Republicans over the lowering of flags at the grave. As a result, they were prevented from reaching the graveside of Wolfe Tone, who had vowed to 'substitute the common name of Irishman for Protestant, Catholic and Dissenter'. The irony was apparent to friend and foe alike. Bodenstown declined as a place of pilgrimage after 1936 when de Valera, now in power, banned the IRA. In 1939, in response to the current IRA campaign, the Government banned all demonstrations at Bodenstown.

1938, Wexford and another Father Murphy

Fr Patrick Murphy, Parish Priest of Glynn, Co Wexford, was an ardent Nationalist and especially interested in the1798 Wexford Rising. Believing that he wouldn't live to see the 150th anniversary of the '98 Rising, he decided to get commemorations under way in his county in 1938. The priest became so associated with the commemoration that he was accorded the epithet '98'. Fr Murphy, like most involved in commemoration in these years, was an adherent of the version of '98 expounded by his fellow Wexford priest, Fr Kavanagh.

The Wexford 1938 commemorations seemed to capture the national mood and were taken up throughout Nationalist Ireland. This was the high tide of de Valera's campaign to dismantle the Anglo-Irish Treaty of 1921. His 1937 Constitution, Bunreacht na hÉireann, had established a 'Republic in all but name'.

In 1938, in an announcement in *Wolfe Tone Weekly*, the IRA Army Council was symbolically designated the legitimate Government of Ireland by 'the faithful survivors of the 2nd Dail' (i.e. the Republicans defeated in the Civil War). The IRA used the commemorations to create the mood music for a further phase of armed struggle, which began at the beginning of the Second World War.

A youthful Conor Cruise O'Brien was a leading proponent of the commemorations, which accorded with his then anti-partitionist politics. The centre of the 1938 commemorations was in the southeast, the home base of Fr Murphy. The largest demonstration that year was on 26 June at Vinegar Hill, attended by some 20,000.[74]

The 1948 commemorations

During the sesquicentenary year of 1948 there were large rallies and parades all over the country, practically every weekend from June to November. Many of the participants were veterans of the 1938 commemorations, and local organisations were reinvigorated and simply dusted off banners and other accoutrements left over from the 140th anniversary. The speeches this time not only referred to '98 but also reflected the concern of Nationalism, north and south, with ending Partition. Mostly this was expressed in a call to England to get out of the Six Counties. The All-Ireland '98 Commemoration Association, based in Wexford, was a major force in the national commemorations.

One of the chief events in the commemorative calendar was the National Celebration at Vinegar Hill, Enniscorthy on Sunday, 20 June 1948, organised by the All-Ireland '98 Commemoration Association. That day, some 25,000 watched contingents from a dozen counties, bearing pikes, march to the summit. Archdeacon Cloney PP, President of the All-Ireland '98 Association, led the obsequies. The Minister for Posts and Telegraphs, Mr Everett, said he was proud to be able to commemorate the men of '98 in the issue of a special postage stamp. Sir John Esmonde SC, TD, said that so long as the invader was within our shores we had not kept faith with the men of '98.[75] Senator Denis Ireland said that the trouble with his fellow Protestants of the north was that they were afraid to think. If they did think they would break down the whole sphere of their unfounded fears.[76]

Fr Patrick Murphy had not only lived to see the 150th anniversary but, as Chairman of the All-Ireland '98 Commemoration Association in 1948, he outdid his role of 1938. He was one of the most sought-after speakers for 1948 commemorations in the south.

At every event he put across, in highly charged rhetoric, a message with as much relevance to the situation in the north at that time as to the memory of 1798.[77] For instance, on Sunday 11 July he addressed some 6,000 gathered at the 'The Croppies' Grave' to commemorate the battle of Clonard, Co. Meath. On that day in 1798, Wexford insurgents had been defeated by the Yeomanry of Lieutenant Tyrrell. Fr Murphy clearly linked the struggle then with that of his own day:

> We would like that these celebrations would result in the linking up of our organisation with the fight for the abolition of Partition as the aims and objects of the men who died in '98 will not have been achieved as long as England holds the lands of the O'Donnells and the O'Neills.[78]

On the same day, at a large '98 gathering at Clonegal, local Wexford Labour TD, Brendan Corish, Parliamentary Secretary to the Minister of Local Government, was on the same message:

> These celebrations throughout the country were a grand symbol of the unity that existed between Irishmen of the present day. There was a danger that Partition was being accepted and taken for granted by the younger generation. This must not happen. The sacrifices made by the men of '98 and 1916 must not be forgotten as their cause was just.[79]

The following Sunday, Fr Murphy returned to his theme at Kilanne, Co. Wexford, birthplace of '98 leader John Kelly:

> The ideal for which the men of '98 had fought and died had not yet been achieved, and as long as England held the North, Ireland was not free. It was time for England to end aggression and clear her armed forces out of the North.[80]

On Sunday 26 July, at a '98 commemoration at St Mullins, Co. Carlow, Fr Murphy reiterated his demand:

> Ireland would not be free as long as a single British soldier remained on Irish soil. England held by force Six Counties which were very dear to Irish people as the homeland of the McCrackens, the Hopes and the McAllisters and other Presbyterian and

Protestant heroes who shed their blood for Ireland. It was time for England to clear out as she had cleared out of India and Egypt. As long as she remained in Ulster, she was a threat to peace and an obstacle to the industrial development of Ireland.[81]

On Sunday, 1 August, a commemoration of the so-called 'Castlebar races', the victory of Humbert and his United Irish allies, was attended by some 20,000 in the Co. Mayo town. Dignitaries representing Church and State included the President, Sean T. O'Kelly, An Taoiseach, John Costello, Mr Sean MacBride, Minister for External Affairs, several junior ministers, the French Minister Count Ostrorog, the Archbishop of Tuam, the Bishop of Galway, other prominent clerics and members of the armed forces. Following a commemorative mass there was the usual round of orations. John Costello alluded to the events of '98 and touched on the anti-Partition theme that in 1948 characterised such speeches.[82] The French Minister placed the commemoration in the Cold War context of the day:

> Count Ostrorog ... said that by the grace of God the Irish and French soldiers who fought together in '98, had never fought against each other. Now the Irish and French Governments had united their efforts with those of other Governments to fight again for the ideals of faith and liberty.[83]

The irony of this is that Humbert, the French commander and hero of the Irish, had in fact been involved in the 'Terror' against Catholics during the French revolution which had carried out mass executions including those of clergy in the Vendée. The event at Castlebar came to a conclusion with a colourful re-enactment of the battle carried out by the army.

A major component of the inter-party Government of John Costello was the left-leaning Republican party, Clann na Poblachta, led by Sean MacBride, son of Maud Gonne. Undoubtedly, this was a major force in seeing that there were officially sponsored commemorative events. Many of these events were virtually Church and State 'con-celebrations', involving prelates and Government ministers, representatives of the rebel counties of 1798 and firing-parties composed of contingents of the Irish armed forces and the Old IRA.

The Father Kavanagh 'Faith and Fatherland' explication of '98 provided a fitting ideological backdrop to this scenario.

On 22 August 1948, the President, Sean T. O'Kelly, An Tánaiste, William Norton, the Minister for External Affairs, Sean MacBride, Éamon de Valera and other dignitaries attended the handing over to the State of the Dwyer–McAllister memorial cottage at the Glen of Imaal, Co. Wicklow.[84] The occasion gave an opportunity to de Valera to juxtapose neatly the themes of '98 commemoration and ending Partition:

> the objective for which the men of '98 fought was still the objective of the Irish nation. Their one desire, whether at home or abroad, was to see their country united and free, and he would like to add, Irish-speaking as well. At that historic cottage the traditions of the Glens of Antrim and the Glens of Wicklow had been brought together as a symbol in which there was no Partition.[85]

Sean MacBride made an appeal to Protestants in the north:

> we extend the hand of friendship to our fellow-countrymen in the Six Counties and ask them to come in and co-operate with us in building Ireland into a truly healthy and united democratic State. If they have any fears we will give them any guarantees that may reasonably be required. We genuinely want their co-operation.[86]

Side by side with the mainstream commemorations, small groups of left-wingers and advanced Republicans, particularly in Dublin and Belfast, took advantage of the commemorative year to propagate the radical ideas of the United Irishmen. The membership of the Dublin 1798 Commemoration Committee was as follows: Chairman P.T. Daly, Vice-Chairman Michael Cremin, Honorary Secretaries Rosamund Jacob, Greg Murphy, Paddy Byrne, Maire Comerford and George Gilmore. The honorary treasurers were Mrs Kathleen Clarke (widow of the executed 1916 leader Tom Clarke), S.G. O'Kelly and M. Wall. Affiliated organisations were Conradh na Gaeilge (the Gaelic League), Dublin Trades Union Council, Cumann na Poblachta (the Republican Club), the National Association of the Old IRA (Pre-Truce), the Republican Congress, Clan na nGaedheal (Republican Girl Scouts), Cumann Oglaigh na

Cásca (Easter Week veterans), Association of Old Cumann na mBan (Women Republican volunteers), Women's Prisoners' Defence League, Thomas Davis Historical Society. The Dublin '98 Committee published at 3d a pamphlet, *'98: Who Fears to Speak?*, with the silhouette of a pikeman on the front cover. This mainly provided a short history of the Rising that rejected the ideas of both Musgrave and Father Kavanagh and their adherents. The last section provides an interesting illustration of the thinking of advanced Republicans and radicals in 1948, not only towards '98 but also to the politics of their own day:

> The heroes of '98 sleep in their graves. The task to which they set their hands has still to be accomplished. Today, when there is so much talk of perpetuating their memory in monuments of stone, let us determine to erect to them an everlasting monument by establishing again the Irish Republic for which they died. And no amount of lip-service paid to them by reactionary demagogues must be allowed to obscure this fact – the United Irishmen of Antrim and Down and of Wexford and Killala visualized an Irish Republic as independent of Empire as the newly freed United States of America, and as truly devoted to liberty and democracy as the French Republicans of their day.
>
> Our commemoration of '98 must see itself as a hosting of the forces that must carry through the unfulfilled task of separating the Ireland of the men of Antrim, Wexford, and Mayo from the British Empire. It must see itself, too, as one of the great armies of all submerged nations struggling to be free. With the United Irishmen we must declare ... that the will of the overwhelming majority of the Irish people is loyal to the principle of an Irish Republic, and just as the United Irishmen called to English democracy we call on friends of liberty in Britain to demand the withdrawal of British troops from Northern Ireland and the termination of subsidies to the Craigavon junta in Belfast.[87]
>
> We declare that the principle of civil and religious liberty which inspired the rising of 1798 is not merely the sentiment of the Irish people but a sacred trust to which the Republic of Ireland is inseparably attached.

Dublin '98 Week

The official 1948 commemorations climaxed in Dublin '98 Week, which ran from 13 to 21 November. The highlight of the festivities was a massive parade through the capital on Sunday, 14 November. The parade route ran from St Stephen's Green to the 'Croppies' Acre'/Esplanade, at Collins Barracks, via Grafton Street, College Green, Dame Street, Lord Edward Street, Thomas Street, James's Street and Steevens' Lane. The route was bedecked with flags, bunting and banners, put up by local residents in co-operation with the clergy and the Old IRA. Some 10,000 marchers took part, watched by 200,000 spectators. The parade comprised 140 organisations, including 2,000 regular troops, the FCA (local defence force), and non-official bodies such as the Gaelic League and the Catholic Boy Scouts of Ireland. Pride of place was given to the Anti-Partition League and the Belfast '98 clubs. While most of the floats and tableaux depicted 1798, representations of other eras, such as 1916 and the 'Tan' war, provided lines of affinity down the generations. Prominent among these was a float depicting the General Post Office aflame in the 1916 Rising. This was based on the famous watercolour by Walter Paget, The Birth of the Republic.

An official tribute was held at the 'Croppies' Acre'. On the platform were President Sean T. O'Kelly, An Taoiseach, John Costello, An Tánaiste, William Norton, other ministers, the Lord Mayor of Dublin, Alderman Breen, Mr Éamon de Valera, the French Minister, Count Ostrorog, and upper echelons of the armed forces. A 21-gun salute was followed by a fly-past of Hurricanes of the Army Air Corps. A 100-strong firing party composed of regular army, FCA and Old IRA fired a volley and the military band played 'The Memory of the Dead', 'The Marseillaise' and the Irish National Anthem. This was followed by a reception in Collins Barrack Square for 700 guests. The guests of honour were the Hon. Brian Fitzgerald, great-nephew of Lord Edward, and Mrs Fitzgerald.[88]

On 15 November, the Round Room at Dublin's Mansion House was packed to hear a lecture on the military aspects of 1798 by Commandant-General Tom Barry of Cork, who had himself been a major figure in that respect during the War of Independence,

1919–21. He also drew lessons for their own day from '98. Barry told his audience:

> If '98 had taught them that spasmodic or badly planned action could not succeed, it had also taught them that if they marched together there was no power on earth that could stop them from liberating the Six Northern counties, breaking the connection with England and making a living entity of the Irish Republic.[89]

On Thursday, 18 November a second parade was held along the same route, this time involving some 20,000 Dublin school and college students who had been given the day off for the occasion. A final rally scheduled for Sunday, 21 November at the GPO degenerated into farce because of a row between two major speakers billed to attend, An Tánaiste, William Norton (Labour), and Sean McEntee (Fianna Fáil). This row had arisen earlier over the debate surrounding the repeal of the External Relations Act and the introduction of a Republic. Seemingly this would be the fulfilment of the main aim of the United Irishmen, at least in the south. For many, the declaration of a Republic fittingly crowned the commemorative year. Nevertheless, as a result of political point-scoring and bickering, bitter recriminations between Government and Opposition ensued.

The watching crowd at the final rally was some 200,000, the same as at the opening march of the week. The number of marchers was 8,000. Pride of place in the march was given to northern '98 clubs:

> Their large-size banners, many of them historic emblems which have been carried at national demonstrations for half a century, were especially noticeable … Heading the advance guard … was St Malachy's Pipers' Band, Belfast, leading the Michael Dwyer and Henry Munro '98 Clubs, Belfast. Then came the Davis Pipe Band, Newry, with the Newry and Glenn districts '98 Clubs and St Lawrence O'Toole band, the IT&GW Belfast Group and the Father Murphy and Wolfe Tone '98 Clubs, Belfast.[90]

Norton didn't attend the rally, though McEntee did and spoke for 15 minutes. There were scandalous scenes involving the booing of speakers and a near riot. Nevertheless, the business of the rally, which was attended by 60,000 people, was carried on. The ubiquitous Fr Patrick Murphy took the final opportunity of pressing home his twin themes for the year:

> never before were the men of '98 so honoured as they had been honoured by Church and State in Dublin during the '98 Week. The ideals of the men of '98 would not be completely achieved so long as a British soldier remained on the soil of Ulster. On the question of Partition and England's attitude towards Ireland, he thought that the time had come for a showdown with England – a showdown to show her up as a barbaric tyrant. England's prejudice against this country was as intense today under a Labour Government as it was under Peel …[91]

Ironically, northern speakers were caught up in the cross-party booing. Mr J. McSparran MP, KC appealed to the crowd:

> We never believed that the day would come that in the precincts of the Post Office we would not be afforded a fair hearing. You may have your own squabbles about external affairs, but do not let them blind your eyes to the real state of affairs. We have had twenty years of an ebb tide and the tide threatens to ebb still further.

Mr V. Halley, Chairman, Irish Socialist Republican Party, Belfast, said that the tradition of violence in Irish politics was a long and honourable one. The frustration suffered in a subjugated country by the most idealistic of its citizens had at times demanded easing in a blaze of action.[92] This speech was far more militant than any made by Halley, a northern Presbyterian, during the September 1948 Belfast commemorations, in which he played a prominent role.

Northern commemorations, 1948

In the north, the 1948 commemorations took place against a backdrop of increasing sectarian polarisation. For the first time since the northern state was set up, commemorations were officially allowed. Indeed, the Unionist Government had previously used Orders in

Council to ban Nationalist monuments such as the memorial to Roddy McCorley, the United Irishman hanged at Toomebridge.

Although still hampered by Stormont's use of emergency legislation, Nationalists were in a defiant mood for a number of reasons. Firstly, the release of wartime internees had raised the profile of the Republican movement in Nationalist areas. The impact of the Anti-Partition League, north and south, made for a more uncompromising mood. Culturally there was a more consciously Irish attitude. Irish language classes and *céilidhe* (dances) flourished in the Nationalist areas. That sentiment was heightened by the declaration of a Republic in September 1948.

The Belfast Commemoration Committee, based in Hawthorn Street off the Springfield Road in Nationalist west Belfast, was largely made up of Republicans, ex-internees and anti-Partitionist Socialists, the last of these being mainly from a Protestant background. The *Belfast Telegraph* wrongly described the committee as 'Presbyterians to a man'. The actual membership was: Chairman Cathal McCrystal, Vice-Chairman Sean (Batt) McArdle, Secretary Joe Deighan, Treasurer Jean McHugh, Trustees Senator Denis Ireland, Cathal O'Byrne, Thomas O'Reilly, Jack MacGougan, Seamus McKearney, Nora McKearney (sister of Seamus), Leo Martin, Victor Halley, Harold Binks, Seamus MacFearain, Tomas O'Raghallaigh, Betty Graham MacDowell, Vincent Kelly, Owen Keane and William Rooney. Of necessity, the full committee list was not generally in circulation and therefore the above may be incomplete. The Committee produced *Ninety Eight*, a commemorative booklet of short stories, articles and ballads, edited by Seamus McKearney. The following extracts from the introduction clearly indicate the thinking of that time in northern radical and Republican circles:

> ... this man Tone and his words ringing clear down through the years are the Gospel of True Democratic Republicanism.
>
> It was the genius of Tone which conceived and nourished the Society of United Irishmen ... Connolly, too, acknowledged the worth of Tone's Doctrine, as did also Terence McSwiney; and Pearse, gallant Pearse, never wavered or lost an opportunity of praising him. Again and again in his speeches and in his writings,

the Example of Tone, the Ideals of Tone, the Gospel of Tone is enunciated: *'That God spoke to Ireland through Tone,'* he says, *'and through those who, after Tone, have taken up his Testimony, that Tone's teaching and theirs is true and great and that no other teaching as to Ireland has any truth or worthiness at all, is a thing upon which I stake all my mortal and all my immortal hopes.'*

... It would be hypocritical to commemorate the men of '98 if we ignore their aspirations: it would be foolish to ignore their aspirations when today as then, our Country and our countrymen stand divided and disunited: when today, in spite of the evolution of social justice, we still fall short of the Ideal State the founders of the United Irishmen envisaged.

Today, as then, the privileged class exists; today, as ever, they resist every attempt to form a True Democracy; today, as then, they have their 'Monsters' their 'Destroyers of Civilization' with which to frighten the people into their wars. Today, as in the days of the United Irishmen, we need a union: a union of all creeds ... of all men ... of all hearts. With that union of men we can confidently face the future; with that union of hearts we can build the only monument worthy of the United Irishmen – A Free and Indivisible Nation.

The committee gave notice of a rally to be held on 13 September at a bombsite known as 'Blitz Square', off High Street. The site was just across the street from the place of execution of Henry Joy McCracken in Belfast city centre. The  rally was banned from the city centre and limited to the Nationalist west of the city by the Minister of Home Affairs, Edmund Warnock. The committee instead organised a march to the Cave Hill, which passed off without incident.

The *Irish News* described the proceedings under the banner heading:

BELFAST'S TRIBUTE TO THE MEN OF NINETY-EIGHT

High above Belfast – at McArt's Fort on storied Cavehill, intimately associated with Wolfe Tone and the United Irishmen and on the spot where the United men took the oath 150 years ago pledging themselves to their motherland – hundreds of nationally-minded people (Protestant and Catholic), last night paid tribute to those Irish men and women who fought and died in the '98 rebellion. It was a meeting to which those who attended had to climb the tortuous and dangerous paths to the 1,100-feet summit of the fort, one of which (the Sheep's Path) was the route taken by McCracken and Tone when they went to take the path not to desist their efforts until Ireland was free.

There was a dramatic moment when, in the gathering dusk and after the first meeting had taken place, the skirl of the pipes was heard and watchers saw a long procession headed by the Tricolour and men carrying pikes, wending their way towards the fort … only three uniformed members of the R.U.C. were to be seen … Mr Cathal McCrystal, chairman of the '98 Commemoration Committee, who presided, said the ban on the High Street meeting was an insult to the citizens of Belfast. They were deprived of the right to do honour to the men who were Protestants as well as Catholics. The Minister seemed to have forgotten that the time was passed when they had the political illiteracy of 1920. Now they registered their protest against the tyranny that brought the '98 men out to give their lives to break the chains that ever bound them to England.

Mr Victor Halley, a Presbyterian and member of the Commemoration Committee, said out of Wolfe Tone and his times had come a memory and a tradition of political behaviour that is ever-fresh in the hearts of freedom-loving Irishmen everywhere. The people who destroyed Tone in Ireland were those who feared the Protestant tradition of association with America, French Republicanism, freedom and democracy. Controlling by legal forms their corrupt and illegal coercion of freedom in Ireland, they killed the physical support for freedom. But powerful as they were, they could not kill ideas … of Liberty, Equality and Fraternity … To unite the whole people of Ireland – to abolish the memory of all past dissensions, and to substitute the common name of Irishman in place of the denominations of Protestant, Catholic and Dissenter – these were his means – these were the aims of the United Irishmen and these would be the aims of a United Ireland.

Mr Jack McGougan, a Presbyterian, ex-chairman of the Northern Ireland Labour Party and a member of the Commemoration Committee, said … Wolfe Tone was the advocate of the new social forces that arose in all parts of the world during that period. And when they paid tribute to the United Irishmen let them remember that they had the closest fraternal links with the democratic forces in other countries ...[93]

After this commemorative ceremony had ended, a separate unsanctioned parade of about 100 Republicans from the Ardoyne and Bone areas of the city, headed by a colour-party and a lone piper, arrived. They held a separate ceremony on the Cave Hill. Present at this event was James Stewart from the Bone, then a 12-year-old boy.[94] The 'Weirs' in this account are actually James Stewart and his family:

> At the entrance to Carr's Glen the marshals formed double ranks. 'We want this demonstration to look as big as possible', one proclaimed. 'We will parade to the old mill, break ranks, make our way individually through the glen, then reform at the low side of the old quarry. We'll follow Tone and McCracken's route along the sheep's path to McArt's Fort. There we'll renew our oaths at the Rising of the Moon.' Then the order rang out and they moved off slowly behind the swirl [sic] of the pipes and the beat of the drum. Jamsey stumbled along between his mother and his sister, tripping occasionally on the uneven surface and sliding into water-filled wheel ruts. They snaked their way along the lane, swung right over a small concealed bridge and into a wide clearing surrounding the ruins of an old mill. The dwelling attached to the old mill was still occupied, and the residents were amazed to see them come. But not as surprised as the R.U.C. men, in the hollow by the burn, throwing sticks at the horse-chestnut trees. When they realized what was happening they rushed towards the parade, buttoning up their tunics as they came. 'Peelers! Peelers!' ran the cry along the parade. Immediately there was a surge forward. The marshals tried to regain control. 'Go around them! Go around them!' they screamed. 'No confrontation, No confrontation!' The peelers headed for the colour party and the pikemen. Most of the marchers obeyed instructions and scattered through the glen. Mrs Weir, Jamsey and his sister moved to the higher ground behind the mill ... In the struggle a pike was dropped and Jamsey managed to get hold of it ... A few of the colour party and pikemen were still struggling with the peelers. Emotions were running high and with

the pike across his chest Jamsey screamed down at the melee, 'I'll pike one of those bastards' ... They could hear the distant yells and shouts of their comrades as they answered the call of the pipes to reform ... Slipping and sliding they made their way round the quarry and into the coniferous forest surrounding the Belfast Castle. By this time Jamsey was sore, tired and very uncomfortable ... The joy of getting past the peelers and their determination to rejoin their comrades made the discomfort bearable ...

Through the stillness the distant sound of pipe and drum reached them. Wave after wave of emotion swept over him. Fear, elation, pride and joy. Was this how it felt on the 7th June 1798 marching over these same hills towards Antrim town, McCracken and his 5,000 pike men? 'Get up Jamsey they're coming' ... They could hear the tramp of feet, the swirl of pipes and then the marchers appeared out of the dusk. The green flag at their head with its gold harp waving a last farewell to the light of the day and rejoicing at the rising of the full harvest moon. It was a dramatic moment when in the gathering dusk they rejoined the parade. At McArt's Fort they pledged themselves once again to the ideals of the United Irishmen. Liberty, Equality, Fraternity and the uniting of Catholic, Protestant and Dissenter under the common name of Irishmen. Word filtered through the demonstrators that police reinforcements had left Bellevue so there was just time to read the 1916 Declaration and close with 'Who Fears To Speak Of '98'. Then it was every man for himself.

In the dark the demonstrators scattered all over the Cave Hill. They slid, stumbled and crawled their way back down through the trees. When they eventually arrived home they were elated.

The '98 Ulster Hall Céilidh

The Belfast Commemoration Committee had organised a '98 céilidh (dance) for 17 September in the Ulster Hall in the city centre. The hall was owned by the Unionist-dominated Belfast Corporation and, predictably, they banned it on the grounds that it would lead to a breach of the peace. The *Irish News*, in an editorial, saw this as an attempt to ghettoise the commemorations in the Catholic community:

It would be a travesty of the aims of the United Irishmen as well as

1798 Celebrations

WED., Sept. 15
'98 CONCERT
St. MARY'S HALL
Commencing at 7.45
John 'Bill' Thompson
Radio Eireann Tenor
JACK BLANEY ... Baritone
BETTY DUFFY ... Soprano
LIAM MAGEE'S Orchestra
Also
Kathleen Ni Houlihan
W. B. Yeats
Produced by J. QUINN
And
Spirit of '98
Script by S. MacFearan
★
RESERVED 3/-
Unreserved (Pay
at Door) 2/-
★
Booking at G. McGowran's,
Bank Street

THUR., Sep. 16
At 7.45 p.m.
CORRIGAN PK.
Fireworks Display &
Searchlight Tattoo
Massed Dancing : Open-Air
Concert : Gymnastic Display
Massed Bands
A Night of Music, Colour
and Spectacle
ADULTS 1/-. Children 6d
Stand .... 1/- extra

FRI., Sept. 17
ALL-ULSTER
★ CEILI ★
ULSTER HALL
Dancing 9 till 2 a.m. with
DENIS COX
Famous Irish Baritone
• COMMUNITY SINGING
• :SPOT PRIZES
• NOVELTY DANCES
• DANCE SCENA
A Ceili for Young and Old
★
Refreshments Available
Fear a' Toighe S. McFearain
LIAM MAGEE'S CEILI
ORCHESTRA
TAILLE - - 3/-
★
Patrons are advised to pro-.
cure their tickets at once.
On sale at usual centres.

an injustice to their memory to convert the present Ninety-Eight Commemorations into celebrations for one particular section of the people. Undoubtedly the action of the Government in banning demonstrations in the centre of the city and confining the procession to the Falls Road area is a deliberate attempt to make it a sectarian celebration. The same policy has been followed by the Estates Committee of Belfast Corporation, which, at a meeting consisting of Unionist members only, recommended that the letting of the Ulster Hall for a Ninety-Eight céilidh should be cancelled.

In spite of ban and cancellation, it is encouraging to know that Protestant and Catholic are working side by side on the Commemoration Committee and that many Protestants intend to take part in the celebrations. There is no need for disturbance or unrest. In other lands, the deeds of patriots would be fittingly honoured by the people as a whole without danger of prohibition or suppression. Those who are paying tribute to the Ninety-Eight men know better than to make a mockery of their name by introducing sectarianism into this week's celebrations.[95]

The banning of the céilidh was clearly discriminatory, and the Commemoration Committee successfully challenged it in the High Court. Indeed, the Lord Chief Justice, Sir James Andrews, awarded costs to the Commemoration Committee. That night the organisers triumphantly went ahead with the céilidh, in a packed Ulster Hall. The *Irish News* reported:

Told by loudspeaker vans that the Northern High Court had removed Belfast Corporation's ban on the ceilidh in the Ulster Hall, sixteen hundred people flocked there last night to continue the celebrations in connection with the Rebellion of '98. The atmosphere was one of complete gaiety ... highlight of the ceilidh was an exhibition by 80 pupils of 10 Belfast dancing schools, who danced a hornpipe and reel, finishing in the glare of a spotlight by forming the figure 98.

Patriotic songs were sung by Denis Cox, the well-known baritone, accompanied by Madame May Reid and Liam Magee's orchestra ... Present were Mr Denis Ireland, Mr Michael Kehoe (Secty. of the Wexford '98 Commemoration Committee) and Mr Desmond Crean of the Dublin Committee. Mr Seamus McFerran was fear a toighe [master of ceremonies].[96]

By now, as well as commemorating 1798, the céilidh had become an expression of defiance by political and cultural Nationalism in the face of what they regarded as Unionist repression.

The Belfast march, 1948

The centrepiece of the 1948 commemorations in the north was a procession on 22 September along the traditional Nationalist marching-route of the Falls Road. Thousands marched and many more watched. The march finished at Corrigan Park, followed by a rally attended by some 30,000. Among the marchers were old men who had marched in the 1898 parade. Banners surviving from the centenary parade were again unfurled. The *Irish News* reported the event under the banner headlines:

TRICOLOUR-DECKED ROUTE

THIRTY THOUSAND AT FINAL '98 RALLY

STIRRING SCENES IN BELFAST

From two o'clock onwards the various contingents who had assembled at Smithfield under the banners of Henry Joy McCracken, William Orr, Wolfe Tone, Robert Emmet, the Hearts of Down, marched along the tricolour-decked Falls Road. The Procession was headed by the Dublin Band of the Irish Transport and General Workers' Union followed by the southern contingent, numbering about 400. The procession marched to the tunes of 'Roddy McCorley', 'Boolavogue', 'Who Fears to Speak of '98' etc. Of particular interest was a car carrying several veterans of the 1898 Centenary Commemoration. Several of the original pikes and swords used in '98 were carried by the men in the crowd. At 3.30, to the solemn roll of drums in Corrigan Park, the tricolour was broken at the mast and the crowd rose to sing the 'Soldiers' Song'.

'ONE THING IN COMMON'

Mr C. McCrystal, who opened the meeting, welcomed the contingents from all over Ireland. 'We are assembled here,' said Mr McCrystal, 'to commemorate the men who gave their lives all over Ireland in the '98 rising, but in particular to pay tribute to that body of Protestants who are forming the hard core for the final fight for freedom.

'The next time that we meet to celebrate the commemoration of '98 it will not be in Corrigan Park, it will not be in the Blitz Square, but it will be to celebrate the unity of Ireland … It is our aim that every district in Belfast will have its '98 club. However they differ in creed or class, they will have one thing in common, the desire for the freedom and unity of their country.'

Mr Michael Keogh of the Wexford Committee, praised the work of the Commemoration Committee in organising the week of Commemoration and spoke of the great obstacles which they had to overcome on this side of the border. Mr Owen Keane, a member of the Belfast Committee, told the crowd '… We have people here today, Protestant and Catholic, from Derry and from Wexford, to demonstrate to Stormont the determination of all that is best in Ireland to achieve Irish unity.' Mr Victor Halley and Mr Leo Martin also spoke. The programme also included community singing of '98 ballads, songs by Denis Cox (baritone), and Miss Betty Duffy and a display of Irish dancing by the McCoy School.[97]

On 18 September, United Irish graves were visited at Clifton Street, Mallusk and Templepatrick and wreaths were laid, in some cases by descendants.

Unionist antipathy

Traditionally, the corollary of Nationalist commemorations was
the hostility of Unionists. In 1948, this reflected their strongly
pro-Partitionist attitudes. Of course the majority of
Protestants/Unionists regarded the commemorations of 1948 as an
entirely Catholic/Nationalist affair. Most had little idea of the
Presbyterian nature of '98 in Antrim and Down. This is pithily
illustrated by Gusty Spence, the Ulster Volunteer Force (UVF)
leader, who was convicted of the murder of a Catholic in 1966. He
recalled that he had attended the Falls Road parade with a Catholic
friend:

> He took me to a parade on the Falls in 1948, marking the 150th
> anniversary of the 1798 rising, and for the first time I heard that
> all the rebels in Belfast were Protestants. We were taught no Irish
> history, so it was very confusing.[98]

Unionists' feeling of separateness from the rest of Ireland had been
copper-fastened by the different experiences of the two parts of the
island in the recent war, when Éire had remained neutral. The
introduction of the Welfare State underlined the benefits of the
Union, making Irish unity an even less attractive prospect. The declaration of the Republic in the south made Unionists even more
determined to remain British.

The sectarianism in both camps came to a head the following
year, in the election called by the Stormont Government. This was
in effect a border poll. The attendant strife, and the predictable
Unionist victory, showed how far removed the current political situation was from the aim of the United Irishmen of uniting
Protestant, Catholic and Dissenter. The subsequent history of the
north has ensured that the attitude of most Protestants towards the
memory of the United Irishmen has remained the same.

At the end of the commemorative year of 1948, the All-Ireland
'98 Commemoration Association issued a statement that, while
reflecting the attitude of many in the localities, sounded a note of
caution amidst the celebrations:

> Owing to the praise-worthy zeal of so many hardworking local
> Committees, with whom we have the honour to be associated, and

to the enthusiastic support of the plain people of Ireland, the Nation has this year made a worthy gesture in honour of the heroes of '98. We feel it our duty to thank all those who gave our Committees their support, including the Government, the Hierarchy, the elected representatives of the people, the Army, the FCA, the Old IRA, the GAA, Gaelic League, National Graves Association, the Trades Unions and the Anti-Partition League. Our congratulatory greetings would, however, be fostering an unwarranted and fatal complacency did we not appeal for a consolidation of the good achieved by the year's Commemorations, and for a further propagation of the spirit which they evoked.

There is a danger, a real danger as we shall show, that the very success of our Celebrations may be misleading, that we may mistake the means for the end. The pomp and pageantry of Celebrations, the erection of worthy monuments, the music and the marching were but means to an end. The end was the perpetuation of the living tradition of our nationality in the hearts of coming generations and in particular in the youth of today. Monuments may become meaningless in the absence of popular knowledge of the events and of the men they were erected to commemorate. We have seen many districts where monuments have been erected at great expense and sacrifice during the centenary year of 1898, and have found that these monuments mean little more to many of our young people than does that of Horatio Nelson to the youth of our metropolis! We have talked with youths and school children during the recent Celebrations, and found that, while they were very familiar with the careers of foreign film stars, they knew next to nothing of the events commemorated by the local monuments of fifty years ago, nor of the heroes of 1798 in their own districts, men of their own race and often of their own kith and kin. Not on our youth lies the blame for this appalling ignorance, and for the apathy that arises therefrom. It is on the adult generation that the responsibility rests. Let us learn the lesson before it is too late. Let us realise that those local pieties, those regional traditions, once the most tenuous strands of our Irish nationality, need our urgent attention. We appeal then to our local Committees to reintegrate our national public opinion through the rebuilding of local public opinion, to recover and perpetuate the local history, and traditions commemorated by our local monuments.[99]

Keeping alive the memory of '98

For many years after 1948, the commemoration of the United Irishmen was to remain the sole preserve of the various strands of Republicanism. In a sense they were preaching to the converted. In the late 1960s, Republican Clubs were set up in the north, invariably named after United Irish patriots: Wolfe Tone, Henry Joy McCracken, Jemmy Hope, etc. After the Official/Provisional Republican split in 1969, the Republican Clubs became the Officials' political wing in the north. To a great extent, the naming of these clubs after Protestant Republicans was part of a fruitless attempt by the Officials to build bridges with the Protestant working class.

On 18 November 1967, after a long campaign by, among others, Kathleen Clarke – widow of Tom Clarke, the executed 1916 leader – a memorial was finally erected to Wolfe Tone in Dublin. This was not at the original designated site at the north-west corner of St Stephen's Green, which, as we have seen, had been 'usurped' by the Dublin Fusiliers' Boer War memorial. Instead it was sited elsewhere on the Green, within the park. The memorial took the form of a statue of Tone, by Edward Delaney, commissioned by the Irish Arts Council. It was unveiled by President de Valera with Tone's descendants as guests of honour and in the presence of the Church of Ireland Archbishop of Dublin, Dr George Otto Simms, An Taoiseach, Jack Lynch, several other Ministers, veterans of 1916 and Old IRA. While this indicated official sanction, there was no military parade as there had been the previous year for the 50th anniversary of the 1916 Rising. There was a small crowd, and the event received scant coverage in the press. The President, having alluded to the fact that the Republic Tone had sought had been established 'in this part of the country', continued:

> It would, of course, sorrow Tone's heart not to have the whole nation united and there are not here today representatives from Belfast of the Presbyterians, those people whom he regarded as the most freedom loving and liberty loving of the whole of our people. Their absence today would sorrow him a great deal, but let us have

the hope and courage that Wolfe Tone had. Let us work to see that this ultimate ideal will be realised.[100]

The UVF adopted an iconoclastic attitude to '98 memorials. In 1969 they caused an explosion at Tone's grave in Bodenstown. In 1971 they blew up the Wolfe Tone statue at St Stephen's Green, though it has since been restored. In the same year they damaged the headstone of F.J. Bigger at Mallusk.[101]

The memory of the United Irishmen was kept alive during the 1970s and 1980s at the various commemorations in June at Bodenstown, involving the Provisional and Official Republican movements, the Irish Republican Socialist Party, the Communist Party of Ireland and Fianna Fáil. There were large contingents of Republicans from the north, where the movement had grown in numbers as a result of the conflict. Speeches at Bodenstown, as well as alluding to '98, reflected the current political stances of various strands of Republicanism and the internecine warfare within them. Indeed, Republican orators at Bodenstown, along with those at the Easter Rising commemorations, have long been regarded as bell-wethers in this respect.

1991 was the bicentenary of the foundation of the Society of United Irishmen in Belfast, and the 75th anniversary of the Easter Rising. The commemorations during Easter Week that year were somewhat muted, in marked contrast to those of the 50th anniversary in 1966. Indeed, the tercentenary of the Battle of the Boyne had been marked the previous year with an equally low-key commemorative programme. One of the most useful spin-offs from the Boyne anniversary was a very impressive exhibition, 'Kings in Conflict', with an excellent accompanying catalogue, produced by Dr Bill Maguire and Eileen Black at the Ulster Museum. Dr Maguire and Trevor Parkhill were to emulate this in 1998 with the excellent '98 exhibition and catalogue 'Up in Arms' at the same venue.

There were commemorative events in Belfast and Dublin in 1991. In most cases they were organised by groups of people who were not avowedly political. In Belfast, the Society of United Irishmen Commemoration Committee was set up to organise events. On 14 October 1991, over 600 people packed the Elmwood

Hall at Queen's University for 'A Brotherhood of Affection', organised by the Society. This was a highly successful commemorative evening of songs, music, dancing, drama and lectures. The programme included 'Belfast – the Background', an illustrated presentation by Fred Heatley; 'The Origins and Development of the United Irishmen', a lecture by Dr Tom Bartlett (University College Galway); 'Ninety Eight', a documentary entertainment by Jonathan Bardon on the background to the 1798 rebellion in words, song and instrumental music; and 'music and set dancing of the period', featuring set dancers, traditional musicians and singers. Those attending the event, in this neutral venue, came from all communities.

In addition, the following programme of four lectures was held on Monday nights during the months of October and November 1991 in the Institute of Irish Studies at Queen's University. On 21 October, former Moderator of the General Assembly, the Rev. Professor John Barkley (ob. 1998), spoke on 'Francis Hutcheson and the Origins of Presbyterian Radicalism'. The following Monday, Dr Seamus Ó Saothrai of the Presbyterian Historical Society gave a talk on 'The Presbyterian Church and the United Irishmen'. On 4 November, Professor Breandán Ó Buachalla (University College Dublin) gave a talk in Irish entitled 'Na hÉireannaigh Aontaithe, Béal Feirste agus an Ghaeilge' (The United Irishmen, Belfast and the Irish language). On 11 November Dr A.T.Q. Stewart (QUB) delivered a lecture entitled 'Reflections on the United Irishmen'.

A group of academics from north and south, who were involved in the major reworking of the history of the late eighteenth century, held a two-stage conference, 'The United Irishmen: a Bicentenary Perspective', on 31 October–2 November 1991. Following the first stage, in the Ulster Museum, Belfast, the participants went on to Trinity College, Dublin. The conference was well attended at both stages and the papers, for the most part, revealed the extent of ground-breaking research into the period of the United Irishmen. A permanent outcome of the conference was an edited collected volume based on the various talks.[102] These events were grant-aided by the Cultural Traditions Group of the Northern

Ireland Community Relations Council, a body set up by Government to foster community relations and explore cultural diversity. The grants were awarded on the basis of the cross-community nature of the events and their organisers. It was an important early recognition of the efficacy of studying and commemorating the United Irishmen as part of our common heritage and history.

At the same time, teachers and the historians of the 1790s and the United Irishmen were disseminating knowledge of the period through the schools, particularly in the north. Gusty Spence's earlier complaint that he was taught no Irish history (see 'Unionist antipathy' above) no longer applied. Indeed, the Northern Ireland History Syllabus, common to all schools since the late 1980s, has a very high Irish component. In the A Level History Syllabus, the option 'Radical Politics', which is largely about the United Irishmen and their times, has been a popular choice with schools. This was largely due to the work of the many '98 enthusiasts among history teachers. Many schools got involved in cross-community visits to sites of United Irish significance. A major feature of this process was the many sixth-form conferences at which authorities on the United Irishmen, notably Tom Bartlett, Sean Connolly, David Dickson, Marianne Elliott, Tommy Graham, Daire Keogh and Kevin Whelan were frequent speakers. These sixth-form conferences were started under the auspices of the Young Historian Scheme, based at the Institute of Irish Studies (QUB), between 1989 and 1992, and funded by the Department of Education. This work was until recently carried on by the Education and Library Boards. Thus an unprecedented cohort of knowledgeable students of the United Irish era was built up.

Preparing for the bicentenary

The loose coalition of enthusiasts from 1991 agreed to reassemble to prepare for the bicentenary year. On Saturday, 24 June 1995, an expedition to the Cave Hill, led by John Gray, commemorated the bicentenary of the United Irish Compact. This was a great success and, in retrospect, was undoubtedly the precursor of the bicentenary round of commemoration. On 27 June 1996, the United Irishmen Commemoration Society (UICS) was set up in Belfast, composed mainly of those who had been involved in 1991. Its aim was to organise and disseminate the commemoration of the bicentenary in 1998. It organised a regular, well-attended programme of lectures at the Linen Hall Library in Belfast (see below).

The distinguished patrons of UICS were: Professor Marianne Elliott of Liverpool University, a native of Belfast, who has done much to inform us on the United Irishmen; two former Moderators of the Presbyterian Church in Ireland and Principals of Union Theological College, the Rev. Professors John Barkley and Finlay Holmes, both also considerable historians; and the well-known local historian of Belfast, Fred Heatley. By 1998, the membership of UICS, residing mainly in Belfast and the surrounding counties, had reached 250. It is evident that the membership is a representative cross-section of the community. In this respect it is typical of the bicentenary commemorations, which, particularly in the north, have been very different in composition and emphasis to those of previous anniversaries. In collaboration with the Cultural Diversities Programme of the Community Relations Council, the UICS employed the present author as an organiser/facilitator of events during the bicentenary commemoration, and ultimately to write this work on historic commemoration and the bicentenary of '98.

Even before the commemorative year began, there were indications that this would be different from previous anniversaries. On 4 August 1997, in the Nationalist New Lodge area, a panel of speakers, mainly from a Unionist/Loyalist background, engaged with an audience from a mainly Nationalist/Republican background on the relevance of '98 and found much commonality. One speaker, Billy Mitchell, a former Loyalist long-term prisoner, is now a prominent member of the Progressive Unionist Party (PUP) – the party with close connections to the UVF. He told how as a boy he was brought by his father to visit the grave of the United Irish leader Jemmy Hope at Mallusk. In his community when he was a youth, there was a cultural memory of, but not a political identification with, the United Irishmen. In the light of the current peace process,

the speaker was of the opinion that the time had come for the res-
urrection of the liberal and radical ideas of the United Irishmen.

On Tuesday, 14 October 1997, a commemoration was held
under the auspices of the Remember Orr Society at Templepatrick
Old Presbyterian Church. Two cannon had been hidden under the
floorboards of this same church for use at the Battle of Antrim.
William Orr, the Presbyterian United Irish martyr, is buried in the
graveyard of the church. In the afternoon a ceremonial installation
of a plaque at Orr's grave took place to background music played by
a lone piper. This was attended by members of the Remember Orr
Society and civic representatives of Antrim Borough. That evening
in the church a talk on the 1798 rising was given by Rev. Dr John
Nelson, a Presbyterian minister and historian, which included
poignant accounts of the trial and death of Orr and of the Battle of
Antrim. The talk was interspersed with Irish harp and uileann pipe
music. This set the scene for a commemorative year in which a
major theme would be the reclaiming by many Presbyterians of an
important part of their history, which had in large part been forgotten or banished from communal memory.

The United Irishmen
Commemoration Society
Facilitation Conference

The society contacted all commemoration bodies, north and south,
and organised a co-ordination conference in the Linen Hall Library
on 7 November 1997. Invited to this were representatives of local
councils, cultural groups, local history societies, community associations, and education authorities. In short, a representative cross-
section of those who would be involved in the coming bicentenary
year attended. The cross-community nature of the gathering was
clear. This presaged the actuality of the commemorations in 1998.
After an introductory contribution from officers of UICS, certain
pre-selected spokespersons from major commemorative bodies
indicated what they intended to do to commemorate the bicentenary. This was followed by like contributions from the floor. This

sharing of information and networking provided a good starting point for the approaching year.

The UICS Facilitating Conference on 7 November 1997 was attended by the following.

- Lucy Champion, Ulster Orchestra
- John Robb, New Ireland Group
- Robert C. Davison, North of Ireland Family History Society
- Linda McKenna, Down County Museum
- Deirdre Armstrong, SEELB Library and Information Service, Windmill Hill, Ballynahinch
- Trevor Parkhill and Marian Ferguson, Ulster Museum, Belfast
- Bernard Browne, Comóradh '98, Enniscorthy, Co. Wexford
- Alice Kearney, Department of the Taoiseach
- Brian Kennaway, Grand Orange Lodge of Ireland Education Committee
- David Lammey and Heather Stanley, Public Record Office of Northern Ireland
- Crónan Devlin, Ti Chulainn, Aras an Phobail, Mullaghbann, Newry
- Keith Beattie, Ballymoney Museum & Heritage Centre
- Jane Hubbard, Causeway Museum Service
- Claire Fox and Doreen Corcoran, Federation for Ulster Local Studies (Doreen Corcoran was also representing Carrickfergus History Society)
- Tommy Graham, Dublin '98/editor, *History Ireland* magazine
- Robert Pimley, West Belfast Historical Society
- Josephine Quinn, Dunmurry Local History & Heritage Group
- Paula Donaghy Newtownabbey Borough Council
- Alan Hewitt, Farset Youth & Community Development, Belfast
- Sean McGrath, Trevor Creighton, Jason Caldwell and Shaun Cassidy, NI Youth Forum
- Eoin Magennis, An Cumann Seanchas Ard Mhaca
- Mai Tracy, 'Remember Orr' Co-ordinating Committee, Templepatrick
- Harry Allen, The '98 Rebellion in the Ards (book project/ education pack), Town Hall, Donaghadee
- May McCann, Women in Politics History Project, Belfast
- Aisling Rennick, Newry & Mourne District Council

- Tom Watson and Linda Greenwood, Belfast Public Library
- Malcolm Scott, Community Relations Council, Murray Street, Belfast
- Breeda McKibbin, Down Community Forum, Castlewellan
- Ian Wilson, North Down Heritage Centre, Town Hall, Bangor
- William M. Young, Ballymena Borough Council
- Gary Shaw, Arts Officer, and Sinead Holland, Community Relations Officer, Antrim Borough Council
- Joseph Nolan, Conway Mill Writers, Belfast
- Louis and Olga E. Dunbar, Ulster People's College, Belfast
- Sean P. Murphy, Roddy McCorley Society, Belfast
- Vivien Kelly, Southern Education and Library Board
- Laura Kwasniewska, Western Education and Library Board
- Sheelagh Dean, South-Eastern Education and Library Board
- Heather Thompson, North-Eastern Education and Library Board
- Roisin Keenan, ADM/CPA Programme for Peace & Reconciliation, Sligo
- Anita Gallagher, Border Counties History Collective, Blacklion, Co. Cavan
- W. Duffy and P. Thompson, Irish National Foresters, Belfast
- James McCabe, The Bartholomew Teeling Society, Belfast
- John Bassett and Damien Brannigan, Down District 1798 Bicentenary Committee, Pamela Cooper, Down District 1798 Bicentenary Committee and Ballynahinch Library
- Sean Vinters, CUP
- Andrew Cameron-Mitchell, Community Relations Officer, Moyle District Council
- Brenda Collins, Irish Linen Centre and Lisburn Museum
- John McQuillan, East Belfast Community Development Agency
- Manus Maguire and Pearse McKenna, Belfast Trade Union Council
- Dick Ward, Elizabeth Ward and Jim Bunting, Ards Historical Society, Newtownards
- Felim Ó Dubhfaigh, James Starkey Cumann Gaelach Ard Ghlais, Ardglass

4

The Bicentenary Commemorations
in the North

United Irishmen versus the Crown forces in a re-enactment
of the Battle of Antrim, in June 1998 commemorations

HISTORIANS OF COMMEMORATION OF '98 would dearly love to have contemporary calendars of the 1898, 1938 and 1948 events. None are extant. At the request of the Cultural Diversities Committee of the Northern Ireland Community Relations Council, this chapter sets out a calendar for the bicentenary, 1998.

The Irish predilection for commemoration is well known. Invariably one side's commemoration is seen as triumphalism or provocation by the other. As we have seen, past '98 commemorations were largely the preserve of Nationalists or Republicans. Furthermore, such commemorations were at times used as propaganda for political campaigns or as recruiting opportunities. On 18 April 1998, at Springvale Training Centre in Belfast, the Social Democratic and Labour Party (SDLP) held a commemorative conference, 'Abolishing Past Dissensions: Perspectives for Social Democracy on the Bicentenary of the United Irishmen'. While the conference address was by the party leader, John Hume, the speakers ranged right across the political and academic spectrums.

Early in the year, a controversial Republican march to dedicate a monument in Roslea, Co. Fermanagh, produced a Loyalist counter-demonstration. After that, interestingly, few commemorative events were organised by Republicans *per se* during the bicentenary year. Possibly this reflected a desire to avoid negative publicity in the light of the peace process, then at a delicate stage. In a rare commemorative outing in August, Gerry Adams accompanied the veteran Republican Joe Cahill who unveiled a memorial to the United Irish Teeling brothers in the Nationalist Poleglass/Twinbrook area. In 1998, unlike 1898 and 1948, there was no major march on the Falls Road. The Michael Dwyer Gaelic Athletic Club did hold a minor march on the road to dedicate its new banner, a replica of the old one, which had been carried in 1898. Another new banner was commissioned to replace the original of the Henry Joy McCracken branch of the Irish National Foresters in Belfast.

The significant difference of the bicentenary in 1998 from past

'98 anniversaries was the involvement of all communities in the commemoration. Unlike previous occasions, the bicentenary commemoration generally was not controversial or politically divisive. Although it is perhaps too early for a comprehensive analysis of why this has been so, some factors are already clear. The widespread involvement of public bodies has been crucial. Once again, the Northern Ireland Community Relations Council (CRC), through its Cultural Traditions (renamed Cultural Diversities) Programme, funded many commemorative exhibitions, events and publications. The present writer is grateful to the council for the award of the Mary Ann McCracken Cultural Traditions Fellowship. The CRC also funded an Outreach Officer, Jane Leonard, to promote community involvement in the excellent 1798 exhibition 'Up in Arms' at the Ulster Museum.

Involvement in the bicentenary sprang from a variety of motivations, political, cultural, and historical. There were many debates and community forums, some involving people from different ends of the political spectrum, to discuss the present-day meaning and relevance of the aims and ideals of the United Irishmen. Thus, Presbyterian Unionists could reconcile their present-day political stance with commemorating the involvement of many of their forebears in armed struggle against the Government. They could empathise with the reasons then pertaining for such action, while being opposed to its present-day manifestations. Unionist unease was raised in some council chambers at the start of the bicentenary year, no doubt anticipating the involvement of extreme Republicans in the commemorative events. The Unionist-dominated Ards Borough Council, in whose area the United Irishmen had been strong, debated a programme of commemoration made up of lectures, tours, re-enactments and performances, proposed by its Community Relations Officer. The local newspaper reported that:

> Councillors also feared the 1798 rebellion had been romanticised
> and that republican views could be espoused on council property
> … the issue had been taken over by republican elements … it is
> something the borough could do without.[103]

Alderman Shannon (DUP), who hadn't attended the debate, was

quoted in the paper:

> The whole thing has really been organised as a propaganda of
> Irishism ... not every Presbyterian supported the 1798 rebellion ...
> Those that did support it were involved in social issues relating to
> landlords, taxes and tithe conditions. They were never United
> Irishmen but were involved in bread and butter issues. Many of
> those who fought in the 1798 rebellion ... were not in favour of
> Irish nationalism.[104]

In fact the Council went ahead with its programme of commemoration with, as in all other areas, none of the feared controversy.

Of course many present-day Unionists would have no sympathy
with Tone's stated aims: 'to break the connection with England, the
never failing source of all our political evils, and to assert the independence of my country'. Others would even argue that this wasn't
the aim of most of those who rose in Antrim and Down. For
instance, one of the most extensive '98 programmes was mounted
by Newtownabbey Borough Council. A leading Unionist
Councillor, Fraser Agnew (and a former anti-Agreement
Assemblyman), wrote in an excellent Council publication:

> The truth is of course that Republicanism or Separatism had noth-
> ing to do with the 1798 Rebellion ... To relate the United
> Irishmen to Republicanism is ... a nonsense. Republicanism and
> Nationalism came after the Union was established and that as a
> clear and direct result of the rebellion and demands for reforms. In
> the north most of the United Irishmen became supporters of the
> Union.[105]

The principles espoused by the United Irishmen in a 'Brotherhood
of Affection', along with the French revolutionary ideals of Liberty,
Equality and Fraternity, are particularly relevant to the current
peace process and few would now take issue with them. The somewhat overworked terms 'inclusiveness' and 'parity of esteem', derid-
ed by some as mere buzzwords, derive from the same philosophical
basis. Now that the bicentenary has ended it is evident that, far
from causing resentment and division as in the past, the commemoration of the United Irishmen and their ideals was something
around which people of goodwill could rally. The commemorative

events provided a positive cross-community focus and meeting point, much in keeping with the times. Many northern cultural and historical bodies used the bicentenary to view the United Irishmen through their own particular prisms. The Federation for Ulster Local Studies held a one-day seminar. Many of the 100 or so local history societies affiliated to the Federation held lecture programmes or one-day events devoted to the United Irishmen.

The Orange Order, which in 1798 played a part in defeating the United Irishmen, showed particular interest during the bicentenary. As early as March 1997, Rev. Brian Kennaway, Convenor of the Orange Order Education Committee, met Avril Doyle, then minister responsible in the Republic for the 1798 Commemoration. He stated that 'We are eager to find out what room she has been left by the Irish Government for the Orange Order in this commemoration.'[106] Of course, many of the Order's Presbyterian members are descended from people who turned out in 1798 as United Irishmen. The Order held an exhibition in Comber, Co. Down, 2–6 March 1998, on the history of the district lodges, with a significant section on 1798. An accompanying catalogue issued at the exhibition, which includes a portrait of Henry Joy McCracken on the inside back cover, gives a brief history of the 1790s.

The Battle of Antrim re-enactment on Saturday, 6 June 1998 was organised by the Ulster Heritage Museum Committee, a cultural body with close links to the Orange Order. There was a massive turnout of participants and spectators. The costumed re-enactors seemed to number as many as had participated in the actual battle. An exciting dramatic recreation of the battle took place, with an excellent commentary over loudspeakers adding greatly to the proceedings. During the bicentenary year, members of the Order engaged in debate with other bodies on the legacy and present-day relevance of the ideas of the United Irishmen. A dinner was held by the Grand Orange Lodge of Ireland to commemorate the 1798 Rising, at which Professor Brian Walker, gave the after-dinner address. This was reported as follows in *The Irish Times*.

ORANGE ORDER MARKS 1798
By Paul Cullen, in Belfast

Supporters of the United Irishmen in the late 1790s who looked to France for inspiration were like the western intellectuals of the 1930s who failed to recognise what was going on in Soviet Russia, a leading historian has said.

Prof. Brian Walker, director of the Institute of Irish Studies, at Queen's University Belfast, said many United Irishmen and their supporters failed to take account of the deterioration of the French Revolution. 'To many people, the descent of the revolution from idealistic aims of liberty and equality to terror and dictatorship made them very wary of importing revolution into Ireland,' he said.

Prof. Walker was speaking at a commemorative dinner organised by the Grand Orange Lodge of Ireland to mark the 1798 Rebellion.

Guests included the Lord Mayors of Dublin and Belfast, the heads of the Irish universities and leading journalists from both sides of the Border.

Too much attention had been focused on the United Irishmen and not enough on their opponents, Prof Walker said.

'The United Irishmen were seen as idealistic and "goodies" while their opponents were viewed as reactionaries and unpatriotic. But there were many sensible people who opposed the rebellion for very good reasons.' These included Daniel O'Connell, Edmund Burke, the Catholic Church authorities and the Orange Order.

By 1795, all the Irish colleges in France and Belgium had been closed and Christianity – both the Catholic and Protestant varieties – was threatened by a number of revolutionary Governments. 'There was a real concern that Ireland could become a French province.' The terrible violence of the rebellion tended to be forgotten, Prof. Walker added. Some 30,000 died in under six months, most of them killed by other Irishmen. This compared to 3,500 deaths in 30 years of the Troubles. 'The vast bulk of troops and rebels engaged in the 1798 Rebellion were Irishmen, Protestant, Catholic and Dissenter', he said.

This contradicted the view that the situation in Ireland was one of long-lasting conflict between Protestant and Catholic, or nationalist and unionist. It also showed that special opportunities sometimes arose in Ireland to create strategic alliances with great potential.

'And it showed that the international dimension was as important then as it is now. What happened in the rest of Europe influences people, both for and against the revolution.'

Prof. Walker concluded: 'Finally, societies which fail to cope with problems of human rights and justice leave themselves open to violent challenge.'[107]

At Hillsborough Castle on 16 May 1998 the Irish Association and British-Irish Association held a Joint Seminar on 1798. The opening speech by Paul Murphy, Minister of State, Northern Ireland, was followed by contributions from Tom Dunne, University College Cork, Thomas Pakenham, Thomas Bartlett, University College Dublin, and the final speaker was Minister of State at the Department of the Taoiseach, Seamus Brennan TD.

Cumann Seanchais Ard Mhacha/Armagh Diocesan History Society held a seminar in St Patrick's Trian, Armagh on 7 March 1998. The theme was 'The United Irishmen in South-East Ulster' and speakers and topics were: Kevin Whelan, 'County Armagh in a National Context in 1798'; Allan Blackstock, 'The Race for the Volunteer: Lord Charlemont, the United Irishmen and the Yeomanry'; Tommy Graham, 'The Shift in Leadership from Leinster to Ulster'; and Daire Keogh, 'The Life and Times of Fr James O'Coigley'.

The United Irishmen
Commemoration Society

The main commemorative society in the north, the United Irishmen Commemoration Society, had an extensive programme of activities and events. The work of the UICS was pivotal in the north during the bicentenary year, particularly in the Greater Belfast area.

'98 News

Four editions of *'98 News: Newsletter of the United Irishmen Commemoration Society* were published and distributed free to members and other interested members of the public. This contained lists of '98 commemorative events, news, advertisements, illustrations, etc. It was very successful in spreading news of the bicentenary and keeping people and groups involved in commemoration in touch. Each edition opened with a chairman's address, which focused on the important issues and ideas underlying commemoration. Eamon Hanna, Chairman of UICS, was succeeded in the bicentenary year by John Gray. Editorials by John Gray in *'98 News* provide eloquent commentary on what the bicentenary was about in the north. The following are extracts from these:

ISSUE 3 –

MAY/JUNE 1998

The bicentenary of the 1798 rising is upon us and in particular of that fatal week in June of that year which saw the smashing of the United Irish endeavour in the north, first at Antrim and then at Ballynahinch. What is already clear is that the bicentenary, unlike the centenary, has been marked on an extraordinarily broad-ranging basis, and across the community divide. This is reflected at a general level by the support of 19 out of 26 district councils in Northern Ireland for programmes of events to mark the bicentenary. More specifically, one can point to a variety of major exhibitions, to extensive documentary coverage on television and radio, to revivals of old plays and the performance of new ones, and to the appearance of an extensive new literature, often dependent on the work of talented local historians.

Above all the momentum for all this has come from the local level, and it is at local level that discussion of the 1790s has created enabling space for debate on issues which still have resonances to this day. What has actually happened has confounded those of our lofty academics in the north who have contributed little to the process of understanding while warning us of the dangers of making the attempt. Certainly, two hundred years after the event, we should be open-hearted enough to remember more than the United Irishmen who fell. Let us indeed remember all of the approximately 30,000 people from both sides, or none, who died in the rebellion and surrounding events. They found a tragic equality in death, in a decade which throughout Europe was marked by extraordinary violence; a decade of high hopes of reform met by repression, of revolution met with counter-revolution, a decade marked by the horrors of total war.

Even now, however, we see no equality in the positions struck by the parties to that conflict. We particularly remember the United Irishmen and women as modernisers, the first in this island to espouse democratic principles, and the 'Rights of Man'. The first too, to identify what remains a fundamental truth; that it is not possible for any one section of a people to secure a real freedom for themselves at the expense of others. Hence their call for a 'brotherhood of affection' and for 'an union of Protestant, Catholic and Dissenter' is one that should haunt us to this day. Yes they were patriots for their own country, but not in any narrow sense. They were also 'citizens of the world' looking outwards to progressive developments elsewhere, notably in America and France, and alongside their own movement encouraging United Englishmen and United Scotsmen.

Culturally they encouraged the revival of the Irish language and of traditional music while at the same time relishing the work of Rabbie Burns and writing their own Ulster Scots verse. They were people with a vision which knew no boundaries. Happily too, new research on the United Irishmen enables us to rediscover their breadth of outlook. Increasingly we can cast aside those 19th century fables of a 'faith and fatherland' rebellion, or alternatively, and particularly in a northern context, of an 'ourselves alone' and self-interested Presbyterian rising.

What then of those who opposed the United Irishmen. Let us regret equally their deaths, but let others if they must, celebrate their agendas; their opposition to democratic reforms only uneasily and partially granted over the following two centuries; their acceptance and encouragement of communal division as a bulwark against change; their retreat from the world into inner fortresses. Certainly following the smashing of a radical generation in 1798, these were to be the dominant themes of Irish political life for much of the following two centuries. It brought freedom of a sort – of the sort to be found while forever defending battlements – but it brought neither justice nor ease, even for the apparent victors.

Time indeed to look again at the one great endeavour in Irish history, to chart a more generous course, and we can do so in the sure knowledge that in doing so we favour the myths of no tribe.

If many Protestants, Catholics and Dissenters embraced the United Irishmen, we know equally that they were opposed by people of all faiths. In that sense the 1790s provided a tantalising glimpse of what ought to be our modern politics separate from confessional identity.

JOHN GRAY, CHAIRMAN
30 MAY 1998

ISSUE 3 –
NOVEMBER 1998

We have particularly commemorated the United Irishmen in 1998 because that is the bicentenary of their rebellion, and yet the capacity of the violence of revolution and of counter-revolution to obscure the actual issues at the heart of their struggle remains.

That is not, with the benefit of a morally laden hindsight, to condemn the fully fledged nature of their revolutionary enterprise which necessarily included the rising. While one might not go as far as the Reverend James Porter of Greyabbey and argue that revolutions are the inevitable mode of human progress (he was hung for his pains), what one can say of his age, and of others, is that bad Governments get the rebellions that they deserve.

One can also say that failed rebellions rarely get the historians they deserve, and in the case of '98 the particular focus on the rising itself has given even greater scope for underestimating or misinterpreting the significance of the United Irishmen, and nowhere more so than in Ulster.

Thus two of the most influential accounts of 1798, although from different centuries, that is Musgrave's *History* (1801), and Thomas Pakenham's *The Year of Liberty* (1969), both devote an insignificant 4% of their content to the north. True that this sidelining fitted well with Musgrave's now ludicrous thesis of '98 as a Catholic conspiracy, or Pakenham's now superseded view of an essentially backward-looking peasant revolt. Yet despite the force of the risings in Antrim and Down, they made, in truth, little strategic impact on the fortunes of the United Irish cause as a whole; they did come too late and they were put down too quickly to make a difference.

Thus A.T.Q. Stewart is in one sense right in his *Summer Soldiers* in suggesting that there were in effect three rebellions in 1798, those in Wexford, Ulster and Mayo. Or, rather, he would have been largely right if he had been speaking quite specifically of the military aspects of the rebellion as it actually occurred, though, even in this respect the omission of events in say Kildare or Wicklow creates an exaggerated sense of fragmentation.

Of course the parts of the rebellion that we do see, were parts of an overall United Irish strategy which failed to come fully into effect, and, furthermore, a strategy pursued nowhere more vigorously than from Ulster. Why else do we find Samuel Neilson in Dublin in 1798 desperately trying to ensure a rising in the capital even after the arrest of the Leinster directorate?

More insidiously the military separation of Ulster can spill over into a self-serving 'we ourselves' interpretation of the entire United Irish enterprise in the north; as one that embraced advanced 'civic' republicanism and, simultaneously, a distrust of Catholics and southerners.

It is an interpretation which owes more to subsequent sectarian dis-union than to the United Irishmen themselves.

And one which faces a fundamental problem; its inability to explain why Ulster rose at all? Indeed one informer did suggest that divisions between Henry Munro and the Defenders at Ballynahinch arose because of Munro's insistence on a Presbyterian Republic – strange indeed given that Munro was a member of the established church!

To push this Ulster alone thesis we would indeed have to re-write history; re-write William Orr's 1797 scaffold testimony in which he viewed himself as dying for 'the persecuted Catholics of Ireland', and re-write Henry Joy McCracken's denunciation of the hesitant Ulster leadership for their failure to rise with Leinster and Munster.

No it will no longer do. Such diminishing of the United Irish breadth of vision in Ulster is on a par, and indeed continues to feed off, the now utterly discredited 'faith and fatherland' interpretation of the rebellion in Wexford. There too events on the battlefield for long obscured the actual radical depth of the United Irish movement.

Now 200 years after the event the pikes, even if not decommissioned, serve for nothing but mementoes, and we, in this bi-centennial year, have rightly avoided the mimicking of military failure, though remembering the huge sacrifices involved. Rather we have pledged ourselves, and in our own time, to further that eighteenth century breadth of vision which still discomforts enemies of progress in Ireland, whether north or south.

JOHN GRAY, CHAIRMAN
NOVEMBER 1998

On 3 July at the Linen Hall Library, Belfast Trades Council and the UICS launched their joint publication of John Gray's *The Sansculottes of Belfast: the United Irishmen and the Men of No Property*. On 4 June, at the Linen Hall Library, the UICS launched a historical reprint of Francis Joseph Bigger's *Remember Orr*. One copy was made available free to members and it retailed at £5, a price made possible by a generous grant towards publication by the Cultural Diversities Programme of the Community Relations Council.

UICS lecture programme

The UICS instituted a well-attended programme of lectures at the Linen Hall Library in 1997–8, held usually on Thursdays at 6 p.m. Admission was free.

SPRING/SUMMER 1997

WEDNESDAY, 19 FEB.,
    Dr Brian Cleary, 'The Wexford Rebellion'
THURSDAY, 13 MAR.,
    Tommy Graham, 'The 1798 Rebellion in Dublin: the Dog that Didn't Bark'
THURSDAY, 17 APR.,
    Dr David Hume, 'The Presbyterian Revolt in East Antrim'
THURSDAY, 8 MAY,
    Sir David Goodall, 'Reflections on 1798 and some Lessons for Anglo-Irish Relations Today'
THURSDAY, 12 JUNE,
    Dr Ray Bassett, '1798 and the Australian Dimension'

AUTUMN 1997

THURSDAY, 18 SEPT.,
    Dr Ruan O'Donnell, 'The Dragooning of Ulster: Counter-insurgency Aspects of 1798'

THURSDAY, 9 OCT.,
> Anna Kinsella, 'The Women of 1798'

THURSDAY, 30 OCT.,
> Sean Murphy, 'The Connacht Republic'

THURSDAY, 13 NOV.,
> John Gray, 'Mary Ann McCracken'

THURSDAY, 4 DEC.,
> Trevor Parkhill, 'The Wild Geese of 1798'

WINTER/SPRING 1997–8

THURSDAY, 8 JAN. 1998,
> Rev. Prof. Finlay Holmes. 'Irish Presbyterianism and 1798'

THURSDAY, 22 JAN.,
> Prof. Kevin Whelan, 'The Politics of Memory: the Relevance of the United Irishmen Today'

THURSDAY, 29 JAN.,
> Prof. Thomas Bartlett, 'Informers in 1798'

SUMMER 1998

THURSDAY, 30 APR.,
> Dr Allan Blackstock, 'Double Traitors: Grattan's Volunteers and 1798'

THURSDAY 7 MAY,
> John Gray, 'The Sansculottes of Belfast: The United Irishmen and the Men of No Property' (jointly with Belfast Trades Council as the annual May Day lecture in Grosvenor Hall)

THURSDAY, 14 MAY,
> Dr Breandán Mac Suibhne, 'Radicalism in the North-west in the 1790s'

AUTUMN 1998

THURSDAY, 19 NOV. 1998,
> Brian McDonald, 'The Monaghan Militia and the Blaris Moor Tragedy'

THURSDAY, 26 NOV.,
> Dr Luke Gibbons, 'Progress and Primitivism: the United Irishmen, the Enlightenment and Native Culture'

TUESDAY, 8 DEC.,
> Dr Peter Collins, 'Commemorating '98 Down the Years'

The UICS has recorded the entire lecture programme on minidisc with the intention of eventually publishing selections from it.

Other UICS events

On Saturday, 30 May 1998, under the auspices of UICS, a walking tour of sites associated with the United Irishmen in Belfast was led by society member and author of *The Sites of the 1798 Rising in Antrim and Down*, Bill Wilsdon. The sites included the following (their original names are in square brackets): City Hall [White Linen Hall]; Donegall Place [Linen Hall Street]; Castle Lane to Ann Street [Artillery Barracks]; Crown Entry (first meeting of United Irishmen); Wilson's Court (Northern Star offices); High Street; Waring Street/Sugarhouse Entry; Assembly Rooms (scene of the trial of Henry Joy McCracken); First Presbyterian Church, Rosemary Street; Cornmarket [Market House] (site of hanging of Henry Joy McCracken); Castle Place [Grand Parade]. The tour ended at Dillon's bookshop, Fountain Street, where participants could partake of a glass of wine while browsing over the large selection of titles on the United Irishmen.

The UICS held coach tours to the scenes of the battles in Counties Antrim (7 June) and Down (13 June), each lasting approximately six hours. These were again conducted by Bill Wilsdon and the itinerary followed much of the content of his book. The Co. Antrim trip included the graveyard at Mallusk where Jemmy Hope is buried; the hill at Roughfort where many United Irishmen assembled to march on Antrim; the grave of William Orr in the cemetery attached to Templepatrick Non-Subscribing Church and the interior of the church in which were stored two cannon used by the insurgents at the Battle of Antrim. The tour ended with a walk around the town of Antrim, pointing out the important scenes of the battle. The trip to Co. Down sites began at the Presbyterian Church at Comber; continued to the reputed killing place of Betsy Gray, her brother and her lover Willie Boal; and moved on to the site of the Battle of Saintfield and First Saintfield Presbyterian Church. The trip ended with a visit to the sites of the Battle of Ballynahinch, including the ascent of Windmill Hill.

On 5 July 1998, John Gray, combining his roles as chairman of both UICS and the Cavehill Conservation Society, led a large group from Belfast Castle to McArt's Fort, on Cave Hill, to commemorate the Cave Hill Declaration made by Tone and the other United Irish leaders in 1795. The work of UICS is ongoing.

Bicentenary events organised by public bodies in the north

As well as the main exhibition at the Ulster Museum, there were excellent exhibitions in Belfast Central Library, the Down County Museum, Lisburn Museum, and the Linen Hall Library, Belfast. Extensive commemorative programmes were laid on by local councils, both Nationalist and Unionist-controlled. Nationalist-controlled Down had by far the biggest in the north, as befits a county so heavily involved in 1798. Other Nationalist-controlled councils such as Moyle and Newry & Mourne had a significant commemorative programme, as did the Unionist-controlled Antrim, Ards, Lisburn and Newtownabbey Councils. In these areas, involvement of their populace in 1798 was a major criterion. Councils elsewhere mounted less comprehensive programmes, particularly if there was less to commemorate in their own particular areas. In total, 19 out of the 26 District Councils in the north mounted commemorative events, details of which are given below.

Antrim Borough Council

Antrim Borough Council had an extensive programme, as outlined in the following extracts provided by Gary Shaw, Arts and Heritage Development Officer.

> The 1798 Bicentenary Steering Committee was formed following a meeting of interested persons and groups on 27 May 1997 at Clotworthy Arts Centre. Their role and purpose was to oversee and co-ordinate a programme of commemorative events and initiatives during the Bicentenary year. The Committee was serviced by Officers from Antrim Borough Council, with the Arts and

Heritage Section assuming a lead role during autumn 1997. It was originally anticipated that the Community Relations Section would develop a commemorative programme but due to staff changes and a delay in new appointments, this was not possible.

The complexity and sensitive nature of issues surrounding the 1798 Rebellion were duly noted by elected members of Antrim Borough Council, Officers and other members of the Steering Committee ... Initial discussions of the Steering Committee examined the nature and type of initiative which would be appropriate to Antrim. Three key areas were identified:

- living history scaled re-enactment of the Battle of Antrim
- historic interpretation of the Battle of Antrim and its context within the 1798 Rebellion, utilising new technologies for presentation
- community-driven educational projects.

Antrim Borough Commemorative Events/Projects,

showing organising groups and societies.
(Numbers attending are given in brackets where available and appropriate.)

1   William Orr Grave marker, 14 Oct. 1997, 'Remember Orr' Co-ordinating Committee
2   'Remember Orr' Evening of Remembrance, 14 Oct. 1997, 'Remember Orr' Co-ordinating Committee, Templepatrick Old Presbyterian Church (church packed)
3   Website launch, 29 Jan. 1998 (40)
4   Bicentenary Schools Tapestry, Jan.–May 1998 (15 workshops, 95 participants)
5   *Battle Lost and Won*, David Hall, Publication launch 27 Mar. 1998 (90)
6   Beginner's Guide to1798 Rebellion (4 week course), Feb. 1998 (15 enrol)
7   Advanced Guide to 1798 Rebellion (4 week course), Apr. 1998 (13 enrol)
8   *The Turnout*, Shibboleth Theatre Company, 16 May 1998 (96)
9   *Printing the Past* – printed book and website, May–June 1998,

Duneane and Moneynick PS (40)

10   Tapestry unveiling – Antrim Courthouse, 1 June 1998 (120)
11   Flare Up 1798 Youth music/theatre, 3 June 1998 (80)
12   'Boul Proota Diggers', music/storytelling, 4 June 1998 (96)
13   1798 Exhibition and Launch – Randalstown, 5 June 1998,
     Randalstown Historical Society
14   Commemorative Plaque – Randalstown, Randalstown Arches
15   'Irish Artists in Exile', lecture, 5 June 1998 (20)
16   Re-enactment of the Battle of Antrim, 6 June 1998,
     Ulster Historical Museums Committee (3,000–5,000)
17   Commemoration service, 7 June 1998 (60)
18   Commemorative plaque – Antrim & District Historical Society
19   Interactive kiosk (456 users to date)
20   Battle of Antrim talk – David Hall, Antrim District
     LOL No. 1,320
21   'United Irishmen' – Linen Hall Library exhibition,
     Oct. 1998 (700)
22   Related schools talks, Oct. 1998 (120)
23   James Hope Talk – Dr John Nelson 14 Oct. 1998,
     Remember Orr Co-ordinating Committee

The Arts and Heritage Service received notification of all events listed above. Although comprehensive, this list may not include all related activities within local communities. Aside from events and projects, other noteworthy developments of this commemoration year in Antrim included:

• Battle map devised in association with Antrim and District
  Historical Society
• Visit and lecture by Mr Bill Canning to Keshcarrigan, Co. Leitrim
• Broadcast media features on the significance of the Battle of Antrim
• Nomination of Schools Tapestry for 'Interpret Ireland Awards'
• Visit by delegation of Local Government Forum for the Arts to view
  project
• Successful application to Heritage Lottery Fund for the restoration
  of the old castle wall/battlement
• Sermon preached at Commemoration Service (7 June) by
  F.J. McDowell, printed in full by local press.

Ballymena Borough Council

1 SATURDAY, 6 JUNE 1998.
An event was organised in Ballymena Town Hall under the
general title '1798 Revisited'. The main speaker, Rev. Prof.
Finlay Holmes, delivered a wide-ranging lecture on the origins
of the United Irish Movement and the impact of the 1798
Rising in different parts of Ireland. The other speakers, Dr
Ivan Herbison and Dr Eull Dunlop, dealt with the United
Irishmen's local impact. The Town Hall stands on the site of
the old Ballymena Market House, which was defended during
the Rising by a small number of 'Loyalists' and eventually captured by the United Irishmen. A plaque was unveiled by Prof.
Holmes to commemorate these events.

2 SATURDAY, 6 JUNE 1998.
An evening bus tour was organised around various sites of his-
torical interest in the countryside surrounding Ballymena.
Included in this tour was a visit to the Moravian Settlement at
Gracehill. Excerpts were read from the Moravian Church's
Congregational Diary for the summer months of 1798, when
the village's normal life was disrupted by the events of the
Rising.

3 THURSDAY, 15 OCTOBER 1998.
A talk was delivered in Ballymena Town Hall by Mr Derek
Collie, entitled 'Some Novels of 1798'. He provided an
overview of some lesser-known novels dealing with the period of
the 1798 Rising. This event was also used to launch a reprint of
the novel 1798 and 60 Years After by J.A. Strahan (pen-name
Andrew James), originally published in 1911, and written part-
ly in Ulster-Scots dialect.

All three events were organised under the joint auspices of
Ballymena Borough Council and the Mid-Antrim Historical
Group. They were attended by a broad cross-section of the com-
munity, including both Unionist and Nationalist Borough
Councillors. No negative feedback was received.

Ballymoney Borough Council

The following information was provided by the energetic Keith Beattie of Ballymoney Museum. Keith has produced a series of excellent comprehensive booklets at £3.50 each: *Ballymoney and the Rebellion 1798* and *1798: an A–Z of Ballymoney and the Rebellion*. These can be obtained from Keith Beattie at the museum. Much of the information in these is also included in a very informative website, 'Ballymoney and the 1798 Rebellion', www.1798ballymoney.org.uk.

Ballymoney Museum holds the following artefacts connected with the United Irish period:

- Ballymoney Infantry yeomanry belt plate (*c.* 1802)
- Ballymoney Volunteers jug
- Ballymoney Volunteers mug
- John Nevin's sword
- John Nevin jug (*c.* 1806)
- three carved wooden 'sansculotte' figures, believed to originate from early nineteenth-century France.

During the bicentenary these formed the nucleus of the 'Ballymoney & the Rebellion' exhibition at Ballymoney Museum, 21 April–28 August 1998 (attendance 542) It was augmented by artefacts in private collections:

- John Nevin's sword stick – Mrs E. Patterson, Ballymoney
- Ballymoney Infantry yeomanry belt plate – Mr T. Young, Coleraine
- Two cloths issued in 1898 to commemorate the centenary – Mr J. Pinkerton, Ballymoney
- Carved coconut, embossed with silver, presented to Magistrate George Hutchinson by a United Irishman whose sentence he had commuted from death to deportation – Peter Hutchinson, Melbourne, Australia.

1998 talks and guided tours were as follows
(attendance figures in brackets).

22 JAN – 'The Gathering' (200)
26 FEB – 'The going' (176)

27 APR – 'The getting home' (109)
3 JUNE –
   The Turnout, a play by the Shibboleth Theatre Group (14)
27 JULY –
   1798 themed walk around Ballymoney (21)
29 JULY –
   1798 themed bus trip around Ballymoney (28)
5 AUG –
   'University of Ulster Talks and Tours: Ballymoney in the
   1798 Rebellion' (16)
30 SEPT –
   'Men of 1798 – Henry Joy McCracken & Theobald
   Wolfe Tone' (51)
22 OCT –
   'Men of 1798 – Richard Caldwell, Alexander Gamble,
   William Caulfield & George Hutchinson' (45)
24 NOV –
   'Men of 1798 – John Nevin, Francis McKinley,
   William Tennant & William Bones' (27)

A radio interview about the commemorations in the Ballymoney area was broadcast on 'Nine Line', Radio Foyle, July 1998.

Belfast City Council

In 1995, an all-party committee of the council recommended that it should support the coming bicentenary. Belfast City Council provided very generous funding to both the United Irishmen Commemoration Society and the 'Up in Arms' exhibition at the Ulster Museum. It is worth noting that this was decided in 1995, prior to the loss by Unionists of overall control of the City Council. Indeed, Fred Cobain, the Unionist leader on the Council, was of the opinion that the climate created in the wake of the ceasefire now allowed Unionists to focus on controversial historical issues such as the 1798 rebellion.[107]

Craigavon Borough Council

The council organised a number of events as part of its 1798 commemorative programme. On Thursday, 2 April 1998 in Craigavon Civic Centre, Dr David Hume gave a lecture on 'The Presbyterian Revolt: Ulster in 1798'. As well as dealing with the events of 1798, this looked at its aftermath and the long-term change in attitudes, particularly in Ulster Presbyterianism. The Council publicity material states that:

> Dr Hume also addressed the question of what happened to the liberal ethos that lay behind 1798, contending that it did not disappear, but was reflected in the political arena until at least 1912, by which time most of the descendants of the Presbyterian rebels were Unionists.

At the same venue, on Wednesday, 29 April 1998, Jane Leonard, Outreach Officer of the Ulster Museum, spoke on 'Remembering '98: How the Centenary of the 1798 Rebellion was Marked'. This lecture drew on the visual archives of the Ulster Museum, including some items from the museum's exhibition on 1798, 'Up in Arms'. In addition, the council organised a trip to the Ulster Museum exhibition, and a 1798 Heritage Trail – a bus tour guided by Dr David Hume. The tour held on 30 May 1998 was so successful that a rerun was held on 12 September 1998. On 15 September 1998, the council launched the travelling version of the exhibition by the Linen Hall Library, Belfast, 'The United Irishmen and the Government of Ireland 1791–1801'. All events were well patronised and received.

Down District Council

Like Antrim, Down District Council area was the scene of a great turnout and battles in 1798. Accordingly, Down organised the largest programme of commemoration in the north. The following are extracts from the Down District 1798 Bicentenary Committee Programme of Events, 1998. This initiative received funding from Down District Council's Community Relations Section, the Central Community Relations Unit and the Down District Peace and Reconciliation Partnership Board.

A WELCOME FROM THE CHAIRPERSON

The Down District 1798 Bicentenary Committee, established by Down District Council, is a cross-community body of representatives from the voluntary, community and statutory sectors. Its purpose is to co-ordinate and publicise a suitable, dignified, and appropriate cross-community programme of events throughout Down District in 1998 to mark the bicentenary of the United Irishmen's Rising of 1798 in Co. Down.

This programme of events is aimed at increasing opportunities for people from differing traditions to develop a balanced understanding and appreciation of the factors and events leading to and during this period in our history.

We are indebted to all the clubs, organisations, societies and individuals who contributed in any way to marking the bicentenary and thank them for their enthusiastic support.

The Committee believe that this cross-community programme of bicentenary events is one of which locals and visitors can feel justly part and proud.

MRS PAMELA COOPER
CHAIRPERSON
DOWN DISTRICT 1798 BICENTENARY COMMITTEE

1998 EVENTS

JANUARY

- Down District Council signage reading 'Battle of Ballynahinch/Saintfield 1798' added to the existing town name signs at the three main roads into Ballynahinch and Saintfield.
- 'The Cause and Course of the 1798 Rebellion in Co. Down', Down County Museum, Downpatrick. A talk by Dr Jonathan Bardon. Organised by Down County Museum.
- 1798 Lecture Series, Adult Education Centre, Downshire Hospital Complex, Ardglass Road, Downpatrick. Organised by East Down Institute.

FEBRUARY

- Tuesday, 3 Feb. and Tuesday, 10 Feb.: 1798 Lecture Series, Adult Education Centre, Downshire Hospital Complex, 7.30–9.00 p.m. Organised by East Down Institute.
- Tuesday, 24 Feb.: 'The 1798 Rising', a talk by John Gray, Librarian of Linenhall Library, Belfast and Secretary of the United Irishmen Commemoration Society. Denvir's Hotel, English Street, Downpatrick, 8.00 p.m. Organised by the Downe Society.
- Friday, 27 Feb.: '1798 in Story, Song and Verse', a history of the uprising of 1798 using stories, songs and poetry of the period. Teconnaught Community Centre, 8.00 p.m. Organised by Teconnaught Community Association.

MARCH

- 'Who Fears to Speak of '98? Should We Commemorate The '98 Rebellion, and if So, How?', A talk by John Gray, Librarian of Linenhall Library, Belfast, speaking in his capacity as Secretary of the United Irishmen Commemoration Society. Down County Museum, Downpatrick. Organised by Down County Museum in conjunction with Down District Council's Community Relations Section.
- 'The Role of the Yeomanry in 1798', Down County Museum, Downpatrick. Speaker: Dr Allan Blackstock (Institute of Irish Studies, QUB). Organised by Lecale Historical Society.
- Launch of book on 'The '98 in Co. Down', Down County Museum, Downpatrick. By invitation. Produced by Down County Museum and the Hearts of Down 1998 Society in association with Colourpoint Press. The Hearts of Down 1998 Society is a co-operative group based at Down County Museum.
- 'The Battle Of Saintfield, 1798', Saintfield Library. Gregg Toner, History Master in the Assumption College, Ballynahinch, spoke about personalities and events related to the Battle of Saintfield. Organised by Saintfield Heritage Society.

MAY

- *The '98*, Down County Museum, Downpatrick. A drama production depicting the events of the '98 Rising in Co. Down performed by the senior pupils of St Macartan's Primary School, Loughinisland. Organised by St Macartan's Primary School History Through Drama Group.

- 'A Ballad for Ballynahinch', Ballynahinch Community Centre. Performance and final judging of ballads marking the 1798 Bicentenary.
- 'Through the Eyes of Our Children', Ballynahinch Community Centre. An exhibition of projects, models, artwork, research, etc. Incorporating a performance that included dance, music, drama, story-telling, poetry and food. Organised by Ballynahinch Primary School and St Patrick's Primary School, Ballynahinch.

JUNE

- South Eastern Music Centre's Down Concert, Down Leisure Centre, Downpatrick. Featuring the Down Junior Orchestra, the Down Junior Concert Band and the South Eastern Music Senior Concert Band. Conductor: Robert Dawson.
- 'The Spirit of the North Is High', Ballynahinch Library. The launch of a source list of material on the United Irishmen and the Rebellion in Antrim and Down. A new SEELB Library and Information Service publication.
- 'Question Time on the 1798 Rising', Ballynahinch Library. Organised by the SEELB Library Service and Ballynahinch Historical Society.
- 'Down with Arms!', a 1798 Commemorative Conference, Down County Museum, Downpatrick. Speakers included Professor Thomas Bartlett, University College Dublin, Dr Myrtle Hill, Queen's University Belfast, Mr Ray Bassett, Department of Foreign Affairs, Dublin, and Dr Allan Blackstock, QUB. The conference also featured a play, musical entertainment, guided coach tours and walks of 1798 sites in Co. Down and a discussion with the contributors to a new book on the '98 Rising in Co. Down. Organised by the Museum and the Hearts of Down 1998 Society.
- Guided coach tour of 1798 sites in Co. Down, departing from Down County Museum, Downpatrick. Organised by the Museum and the Hearts of Down 1998 Society.
- *The Turnout*, Down Civic Arts Centre. A play by the Shibboleth Theatre Co. There are hundreds of stories of the events of 1798. This production takes a fresh look at the rebellion, focusing on three women whose lives and deaths illuminate the nature of this peculiar time. Organised by the Arts Section, Down County Museum.
- A Flower Festival on the theme of Peace and Reconciliation through the Love of God, Magheradroll Parish Church, Ballynahinch (Battle of Ballynahinch 1798 Parish Church). Organised by Magheradroll

Parish Church. Directed by Rev. William McMillan NIGFA and Comber Flower Club.

- 'Who Fears to Speak', Old School, Dunsford. Weekend of Culture in Irish and English. Set dancing, Irish dancing, guest speaker on Down and 1798, and Interdenominational Service. Organised by Cumann Gaelach Ard Ghlais.
- 'Children Together in 1798', War Memorial Hall, Crossgar. Children dressed in clothes, played with toys and sampled food from the 1798 period. Organised by Crossgar Community Playgroup.

JULY

Guided Coach Tour of 1798 Sites in Co. Down. Departing from Down County Museum, Downpatrick. Organised by the Museum and the Hearts of Down 1998 Society.

AUGUST

- Guided Coach Tour of 1798 Sites in Co. Down. Departing from Down County Museum, Downpatrick. Organised by the Museum and the Hearts of Down 1998 Society.
- *The Last Journey of Thomas Russell*, Down County Museum, Downpatrick. A play by Philip Orr. Organised by Down County Museum and the Hearts of Down 1998 Society.

SEPTEMBER

The Last Journey of Thomas Russell, Down County Museum, Downpatrick. A play by Philip Orr. Organised by Down County Museum and the Hearts of Down 1998 Society.

OCTOBER

Lecture on the Life of Thomas Russell, Thomas Russell Gaelic Club, Downpatrick. Organised by Russell Gaelic Union.

EXHIBITIONS

- 'When Down Was Up!', Down County Museum, Downpatrick. Organised by the Down County Museum.

- 'Battle of Ballynahinch 1798', Ballynahinch Library. A display by The High School and St Colman's High School, Ballynahinch. Organised by St Colman's High School and The High School, Ballynahinch.
- 'Background to the 1798 Rising', Ballynahinch and Saintfield Libraries. Organised by the SEELB Library Service in conjunction with Horace Reid and Dr Bailie.
- 'Women of '98', travelling exhibition in SEELB Libraries.
- *The Northern Star* (the newspaper of the United Irishmen). Travelling exhibition in SEELB Libraries.
- 1798 Ceramic Mural Exhibition, Down Civic Arts Centre, Downpatrick. A ceramic project involving three schools in the Down District Council area. Organised by Down District Council's Arts and Community Relations Sections and SEELB.
- 'Through the Eyes of Our Children', Ballynahinch Library. An exhibition of projects, models, artwork, research, etc. Organised by Ballynahinch Primary School and St Patrick's Primary School, Ballynahinch.
- 'Killyleagh and 1798 – Town and People', Killyleagh Branch Library. A display of material relating Killyleagh in 1798 with the people of the area – townspeople, yeomen and Volunteers. Organised by Killyleagh Branch of the North of Ireland Family History Society.
- 'Ballynahinch in 1798', Assumption Grammar School, Ballynahinch. An exhibition of pupils' work on Ballynahinch in the 1790s, with special emphasis on the battle itself. Organised by Assumption Grammar School History Department.
- 'Topographical Maps and Illustrations of 1798', Ballynahinch Library. Organised by Ballynahinch Primary School and St Patrick's Primary School, Ballynahinch.
- 'The Battle of Ballynahinch, 1798', Ballynahinch and Saintfield Libraries. Organised by the SEELB Library Service in conjunction with Horace Reid and Dr Bailie.

COMPETITIONS

'A Ballad For Ballynahinch': a competition to find an original ballad composed in 1998 to mark the Bicentenary Commemoration of 1798. The competition is open to persons residing in or attending school or college in Down District. Organised by Councillors Harvey Bicker and Anne McAleenan and Mrs Elizabeth Bicker.

OTHER ATTRACTIONS

Down County Museum produced illustrated pamphlets, 'Walk about Saintfield' and 'Walk about Ballynahinch', which contain information about the area in 1798. A lasting commemoration of the events in '98 in Ballynahinch is provided by the 'Ballynahinch 1798 Mural Trail': four murals commissioned by a local group, 'Murals Make Ballynahinch Beautiful' (convenor Dr R.B. Henderson). Done under the direction of artist Neil Shawcross, with historical information by local historian Horace Reid, these gable wall murals, which are situated in and around Windmill Street, were unveiled in August 1997. *Betsy Gray*, showing the heroine against a backdrop based on the events of the '98 battle, and *The Blacksmith*, a representation of Matt McClenaghan beating out pike-heads, were done by Bill Gatt. *Four Churches* and *Wind and Water* are the work of Ian Morrow. The Ballynahinch murals are reproduced in the Down District 1798 Bicentenary Committee's Programme of Events '98.

Lisburn Borough Council

On 26 June 1798, Henry Munro, a linen draper in the town, the leader of the insurgents at the battle of Ballynahinch, was hanged at the Market House, the building that now houses Lisburn Museum and Irish Linen Centre. A 1798 exhibition was held in the Irish Linen Centre and Lisburn Museum from March to December 1998. The council brochure set the scene for commemoration:

> In Lisburn support for the United Irishmen came from all classes and from members of the Church of Ireland and Presbyterians as well as from Catholics … Using contemporary militaria, ceramics, and other period objects, the exhibition depicts the story of the events around the 1798 rebellion and its significance for the people of Lisburn and the Lagan Valley.

On 8 May 1998 there was a 'dramatical reading' at Hillsborough Courthouse of John Gray's *Billy Bluff and Squire Firebrand*. On 6 June a pageant was held at the Market Square, scene of the execution, at which the testimony of Munro and the expressions of the sorrow of his family were read. These were followed by what was described in the Council brochure as 'stories of the battle days and the talk of the people's fight'. There were guided historical walking tours, with a 1798 theme, around Lisburn town centre on 13, 20 and 27 June 1998. On 3 October, in the Irish Linen Centre and Lisburn Museum, the Council bicentenary programme of commemoration concluded with a recital of music presenting a flavour of the eighteenth century, by Clare Blake and Frank King, violin and piano.

Moyle District Council

This council, in north-east County Antrim, had a considerable commemorative programme. This opened at the Council's Sheskburn House on 6 March 1998 with a lecture by John Gray, 'Who Fears to Speak of '98? Should We Commemorate the '98 Rebellion, and if So, How?'

On 24 April, in Sheskburn, Trevor Parkhill gave a lecture entitled, 'The Wild Geese of '98: Emigrés of the Rebellion'. The next day, in Rathlin Parochial Hall, Wallace Clark gave a talk on 'Rathlin in the Eighteenth Century'. On 8 May in Sheskburn, Alex Blair spoke on '1798 in Ballymoney and Surrounding Districts'.

On 12 August, at Ballycastle Museum, Dr Cahal Dallat spoke on '1798 in Ballycastle and Co. Antrim'. On 4 September in Sheskburn, Dr Peter Collins spoke on 'Commemorating 1798 Through the Years'. The lecture series concluded on 16 October in Sheskburn, with Rev. Prof. Finlay Holmes on 'The Presbyterians in 1798'.

Other events included a 1798 Exhibition from 21 May to 30 September, which is now permanently on display at the museum. In the drama and music programme, *The Turnout* was performed at Sheskburn on 5 June by Shibboleth Theatre, who also gave 'History through Drama' workshops to secondary school pupils. On 22 May in the Royal Hotel, Ballycastle (part of the Northern Lights Festival) and on 3 June in Bushmills Community Centre, *Boul Proota Diggers* was performed by four Co. Antrim performers, Liz Weir, Willie Drennan, Bob Speares and Billy Teare. On 26 June *The*

Life of Mary Ann McCracken was performed through music, song and drama by Jane Cassidy. Pauline Russell, Community Relations Officer, Moyle District Council, reported that most events were well attended.

Newry & Mourne District Council

The council had an extensive commemorative programme in 1998, as follows.

FRIDAY, 13 MAR.:
> John Gray, 'Why We Should Speak of '98', Canal Court Hotel, Newry.

FRIDAY, 3 APR.:
> Professor Thomas Bartlett, 'Informers in 1798', Newry Arts Centre.

FRIDAY, 24 APR.:
> Professor Kevin Whelan, 'Ideals of 1798', Crossmaglen Community Centre. Kevin Murphy, 'County Armagh and 1798', Newry Shamrocks Social Club.

FRIDAY, 15 MAY:
> Breandán Mac Suibhne, 'The Origins of Uniting in Ulster', Canal Court Hotel.

FRIDAY, 29 MAY:
> Daire Keogh, 'The Life and Times of Fr James Quigley', Canal Court Hotel.

FRIDAY, 12 JUNE:
> Dr Ruan O'Donnell, 'Martial Law and Transportation', Canal Court Hotel.

FRIDAY, 26 JUNE:
> Kevin Murphy, 'The Thomas Lappin Story and 1798 in the Area', Welcome Inn, Forkhill.

FRIDAY, 21 AUG.:
> Dr Finlay Holmes, 'The Role of Presbyterianism in 1798', Kilkeel Town Hall.

FRIDAY, 25 SEPT.:
> Anthony Russell and Ross Chapman, 'Beyond the Battle, Newry and Mourne in 1798', Canal Court Hotel.

Camloch Living History Society held lectures in that village on various aspects of 1798.

DRAMA – THEATRE PRODUCTIONS

- *Henry Joy McCracken* by Centre Stage, Newry Town Hall, Saturday, 7 Mar.
- *Northern Star*, directed by Sean Hollywood and performed by an amalgamation of local drama groups, Newry Arts Centre, 5–7 Mar.
- Tí Chulainn's interactive drama *After the Slaughter*, Newry Arts Centre, Tuesday, 17 Mar. This drama toured local schools throughout 1998 as part of the 1798 Rebellion celebrations.
- *Cill Brónaí*, a musical drama by Kathleen O'Farrell, November.

MUSIC

- Irish Philharmonic Choir performed Mozart's *Requiem* and the songs associated with 1798, end of June, St Catherine's Dominican Church, Dominic Street, Newry.
- Comhaltas Ceoltóirí Éireann branches based in the Newry & Mourne and Dundalk areas held a concert as part of the 1798 celebrations.

MEDIA

Radió an Iúr broadcast throughout the month of October.

EXHIBITION

An exhibition based in Newry Arts Centre began in June 1998.

PUBLICATIONS

Throughout 1998 the *Newry Reporter* published articles by the late Joseph Connellan (MP for Armagh South 1929–33 and Down South 1949–67).

South Armagh Events/ Imeachtaí Ard Mhacha Theas

- Aisling na Tíre Walking Group/Fleá Cheoil Thí Chulainn Thomas Lappin Historical Pageant:
FRIDAY, 26 JUNE 1998, 8.30 p.m. –
'The Thomas Lappin Story and 1798 in the Area' by Kevin Murphy,

Welcome Inn, Forkhill.

SATURDAY, 27 JUNE, 2.00 p.m.,

Carrive Resource Centre – 'A Three-Part Drama Enactment' followed the Lappin Trail to the Craig-dhu where the pikes were made, to the Market Stone where Jemmy Hope administered the United Irishmen oath, to Belmont Barracks and the Whipping Lane where Captain Farnon flogged Thomas Lappin to death.

SUNDAY, 28 JUNE, 12 p.m. –

Lecture: 'An Overview of 1798', Áras an Phobail, An Mullach Bán.

Friday, 2 Oct.–Sunday, 4 Oct., Sliabh Gullion Festival of Traditional Singing, Welcome Inn, Forkhill:

SATURDAY, 3 OCT., 11.30 a.m. –

'The 1798 Songs of County Antrim' by Mr John Moulden. Mr Moulden, a native of Co. Antrim, is one of the most respected collectors of songs in these islands. His lecture explored the songs that originated in Antrim in 1798, and how these differ from those composed during the following centuries to commemorate the 1798 Rebellion.

SATURDAY, 3 OCT., 12.30 p.m. –

'The 1798 Songs of County Wexford' by Paddy Berry. Mr Berry, a native of Co. Wexford and a noted singer and collector, examined the songs of Wexford composed and sung during the era of the 1798 Rebellion.

Comóradh '98, Caisleán Ruairí,
31 Iúil–3 Lúnasa
(Rostrevor, 31 July–3 August)

Organised by the Tom Dunn Society (Patron, Mary McAleese, President of Ireland; Patrún, Máire Mhic Giolla Íosa, Uachtarán na hÉireann)

2 August marked the 200th anniversary of the death of Tom Dunn, hedge-school teacher and leader of the United Irishmen in the Kilbroney area. The following programme of events was to honour his memory.

DE hAOINE, 31 IÚL/FRIDAY, 31 JULY

- Welcoming address – Anthony Russell, Chairman, Newry and Mourne '98 Committee
- 10.30 a.m. – Keynote lecture, John Gray, Chief Librarian, Linen Hall Library, Belfast
- 1.30 p.m. – 'The French Connection', recital by Dr Eibhlis Farrell (violin) and Ros Ní Dhubháin (soprano), Glenside Inn.
- 3.00 p.m. – 'The Liberty Tree', open forum. Contributors included Tommy Sands, Dr John Robb and Councillor Harvey Bicker.
- 4.30 p.m. – 'Who Fears to Speak?' An introduction to the songs of '98, Siubhán Ó Dubháin.
- 7.30 p.m. – 'A message from George Washington', Dr Chris Cahill, Professor Richard Chrisman and other American contributors.
- 9.00 p.m. – 'Crann na saoirse' ('Liberty tree') le Cór Chonradh na Gaeilge agus cairde, Kilbroney Bar.

DÉ SATHAIRN, 1 LÚNASA/SATURDAY, 1 AUGUST

- 10.00 a.m. – Guided tour of sites associated with '98, including Dunn's Barn, the Trooper's Bed and Alt na gCuinneog.
- 1.30 a.m. – 'Mozart and His Contemporaries', song recital with Deirdre Grier-Delaney and guests, Glenside Inn.
- 2.30 p.m. – Guest lecture, Dr Ciaran Brady.
- 4.30 p.m. – Guest lecture, 'Fr James Quigley', Monsignor Raymond Murray.
- 7.30 p.m. – Arno's Vale Dinner: a reconstruction of the dinner held in August 1792 at which Wolfe Tone was guest of honour. Period dress. Guest speaker: Dr Martin Mansergh. Arno's Vale.

DÉ DOMHNAIGH, 2 LÚNASA/SUNDAY, 2 AUGUST

- 10.30 a.m. – Aifreann, le Cór na nOg, Caisleán Ruairí, St Mary's Church. I gcuimhne orthu siúd a fuair bás in '98/In memory of those who died in '98.
- 11.30 a.m. – Visit to the grave of Tom Dunn, Kilbroney Churchyard, on the 200th anniversary of his death.
- 2.30 p.m. – 'The Liberty Tree', an open-air dramatic pageant through the streets of Rostrevor, featuring visiting Wexford pikemen.
- 5.00 pm – 'Master Tom Dunn' – the man behind the myth. Local contributors.
- 7.00 p.m. – 'The Liberty Tree', repeat performance/athleiriú.

- 9.00 p.m. – 'Dunn's Night Celebration', songs and stories of '98 with porter and champ, with the Brotherhood of Tom Dunn: Captain Farrell, the Cobbler McChesney, Citizen Sands, Pike Sergeant Arthur Murphy and comrades. The Kilbroney Bar.

Siubhán Ó Dubháin is also known as historical novelist Kathleen O'Farrell, whose books are set in South Down during the era of the United Irishmen. She is an authority on seventeenth-century opera and an accomplished musician. She is responsible for the historical background and liner notes on the CD *Who Fears to Speak?*, with the Irish Philharmonic Choir and Orchestra.

> Tom Dunn embodied the nobility of the common man, his humanity and courage in the face of hardship and cruelty.
>
> CARDINAL TOMÁS Ó FIAICH, ROSTREVOR, 1988

An accompanying exhibition on Newry & Mourne in 1798 opened in Newry Arts Centre in June 1998.

Newtownabbey Borough Council

The following events were held at the Courtyard Theatre, Ballyearl in 1998.

WEDNESDAY, 6 MAY –
Rev. John Nelson, minister of the Old Presbyterian Church at Ballycarry gave a talk, 'Presbyterians and 1798', which concentrated on the Larne, Ballyclare, Carrickfergus and Ballycarry areas.

THURSDAY, 21 MAY –
the Ballyclare and District Historical Society, together with the Abbey Historical Society and Larne Drama Circle, presented '1798 in the Six Mile Valley'. Using the actual words of Mary Ann McCracken, Jemmy Hope, William Orr, Wolfe Tone, the historian M'Skimin and many others, interwoven with contemporary sources, this spoken narrative told the story of the rising in Ballyclare, Ballyeaston, Ballynure, Doagh and other parts of what is now the Borough of Newtownabbey.

WEDNESDAY, 27 MAY –
a debate was held with the theme 'What 1798 Means to Me'.

Speakers were writer and broadcaster Jane Cassidy, Councillor Mark Langhammer, historian Archie Reid, and in the chair was the present writer.

MONDAY, 1 JUNE –
Shibboleth Theatre Group performed *The Turnout*.

TUESDAY, 2 JUNE –
historian Brendan Clifford gave a lecture, 'Why Rev. Steel Dickson Has Been Forgotten'.

WEDNESDAY, 3 JUNE –
Jane Cassidy and Maurice Leyden performed their popular musical narrative 'Mary Anne', telling the story of Mary Anne McCracken.

THURSDAY, 4 JUNE –
historian Jonathan Bardon lectured on 'The Causes and Course of the 1798 Insurrections in Ireland'.

FRIDAY, 5 JUNE –
pupils from Mallusk Primary School presented 'The Story of 1798 in Newtownabbey', produced in association with History Through Drama, a professional company that mainly works with schoolchildren. Immediately afterwards, a lecture on 'Republicanism: Valid or Invalid?' was delivered by Newtownabbey Councillor Fraser Agnew. This in turn was followed by the launch of the video *The Life and Times of Jemmy Hope*, produced by the audiovisual department of Farset Youth and Community Development Ltd, Belfast.

SUNDAY, 14 JUNE –
Archie Reid conducted a walk through the story of the Battle of Antrim.

SUNDAY, 26 JULY –
historian Dr David Hume led a tour of the old churchyard at Ballycarry.

The beautifully illustrated and informative *The Liberty Tree: the Story of the United Irishmen in and around the Borough of Newtownabbey* (ed. Archie Reid) was produced under Council auspices.

The Council received a lot of very positive evaluation and feedback. For example:

> I congratulate the Council on the arrangements to commemorate 1798. I attended all the events at Ballyearl and found them stimulating and informative.
>
> I commend the Council for their initiative in putting on the

programme, issuing such an attractive brochure and publishing *The Liberty Tree* – Heartiest Congratulations.

I wish to compliment the organisers of the 1798 Coach Tour, it was excellent, well organised and thoroughly interesting.

I would like to congratulate the Council on the excellent way the 1798 Bicentenary commemoration was handled. A delicate subject was handled with great sensitivity and I was extremely proud of the excellence of the advance publicity brochure.

It was obvious that a tremendous amount of thoughtful planning had gone into the various lectures and seminars.

The book *The Liberty Tree* is a credit to our Council.

Congratulations on the excellent programme put on by Newtownabbey Borough Council to commemorate the 1798 uprising – it was diverse, informative, thought-provoking and of an extremely very high standard – well done to all the organisers.

Strabane Council

In this area, the 1998 commemorations of 1798 included the following.

TUESDAY, 24 MARCH –
performance of Jack Loudan's *Henry Joy McCracken* by Centre Stage.
* Strabane Historical Society lecture, 'The Rev. James Porter' by John Gray, Linen Hall Library.
* As part of the Ulster Museum's outreach, Trevor Parkhill and Jane Leonard delivered lectures in a programme that culminated in a visit to the museum by the Historical Society.
* John Dooher of the Strabane Historical Society wrote a 30-page article on events in 1798 in the Strabane area, and concluded: 'The Rebellion period thus passed off without major incident locally.'

Other bodies and events in the north

Other public bodies put on bicentenary events in the north. The Environment and Heritage Service of the Department of the Environment of Northern Ireland held an exhibition at its headquarters in Hill Street, Belfast on the many sites with connections to 1798, including many in State care. These are detailed in a comprehensive accompanying leaflet, *The 1798 Rebellion in Ulster*, which provides a history of the rising in Co. Antrim, Co. Down and Belfast and includes illustrations and brief accounts of relevant places, as follows.

- In Co. Antrim – Cave Hill, Craigrogan Fort, Templepatrick Meeting House, the Courthouse and Masserene Castle, All Saints Parish Church and its graveyard, Antrim Town, Harryville Motte and Bailey, Ballymena and Lisburn Market House (now the Irish Linen Centre and Lisburn Museum) where Henry Munro, leader of United Irishmen at the Battle of Ballynahinch, was hanged.
- In Co. Down – the Market House, Newtownards, Grey Abbey graveyard, Saintfield First Presbyterian Church, Killyleagh Castle, Montalto House and demesne, Edenavaddy Hill and Windmill Hill, Ballynahinch, Annadorn Dolmen and Downpatrick Jail (now Down County Museum).
- In Belfast – the Assembly Rooms (now Northern Bank, Waring Street), Clifton House, Clifton Street Cemetery, Pottinger's Entry, Joy's Entry, Wilson's Court, White's Tavern, Winecellar Entry (all off High Street), First Presbyterian Church, Rosemary Street, and St Mary's Chapel lane.

EXHIBITIONS

- The Linen Hall Library held an exhibition, 2 January–28 February 1998, showing contemporary printed and manuscript sources from its extensive collection.
- The '98 exhibition at Belfast Central Library was based on the existing resources of the library, particularly the Francis Joseph Bigger Collection, and editions of *Northern Star* and *Cox's Magazine*. As well as printed and manuscript exhibits it included artefacts such as commemorative handkerchiefs and ceramics from the 1898 centenary.
- An exhibition, '1798 in Co Down', ran in Down County Museum, Downpatrick from 30 March to December 1998.
- Lisburn Museum and Irish Linen Centre (see Lisburn programme of events above).
- By far the largest exhibition in the north was the Ulster Museum's 'Up in Arms: the 1798 Rebellion in Ireland, a Bicentenary Exhibition', from 3 April to 31 August 1998. It featured: around 300 original objects of the period; important and rarely seen paintings; etchings and illustrations from Ireland, Great Britain and

France; maps, flags and uniforms; and audiovisual presentations. As well as a huge attendance from the general public, the museum facilitated out-of-hours visits from many groups as part of its community outreach programme organised by Jane Leonard. A lavishly illustrated companion volume was compiled and written by historian Bill Maguire, based largely on the exhibits. The museum laid on the following extensive programme of events to accompany the exhibition.

ULSTER MUSEUM
'98 EVENTS

SUNDAY, 5 APR., 3.00 p.m. –
'The 1798 Rebellion in Ireland', illustrated talk, Trevor Parkhill, Keeper of History, Ulster Museum.
SATURDAY, 25 APR., 10.00 a.m.–4.30 p.m. –
'Depicting '98' conference on the visual legacy of 1798:
  • Eileen Black, Curator of Fine Art, Ulster Museum – 'Volunteer and Rebellion Paintings in the "Up in Arms" exhibition'
  • Brian Ferran, Director, Arts Council of Northern Ireland – 'The Betsy Gray Sequence of paintings (1976–77)'
  • Nuala Johnson, Queen's University Belfast – '1798 Monuments in County Wexford'
  • Jane Leonard, Exhibition Outreach Officer, Ulster Museum – '1798 Banners, Murals and Monuments Commissioned in Ulster, 1898–1998'.
SUNDAY, 10 MAY, 3.00 p.m. –
Trevor Parkhill, Keeper of History, Ulster Museum, 'The Wild Geese of '98. What became of the United Irishmen who survived the Rebellion?'. Illustrated talk exploring the fortunes of those who were exiled to America, Australia and Europe.
SATURDAY, 16 MAY, from 2.00 p.m. –
'Paint a Battle', children over eight years of age come along and help paint a mural based on Thomas Robinson's painting, *The Battle of Ballynahinch*.
SUNDAY, 17 MAY, from 2.30 p.m. –
'Paint a Battle', another chance for children to help paint the mural.
SUNDAY, 17 MAY, 3.00 p.m. –
Dr Ruan O'Donnell, St Patrick's College, Drumcondra, Dublin, 'Counter-Insurgency in Ulster, 1797–99', talk on the impact of martial law, imposed in March 1797, and the subsequent course of the Rebellion in Ulster.

SUNDAY, 24 MAY, 3.00 p.m. –
 Tom Wylie, Curator of Militaria, Ulster Museum, 'The Uniforms
 and Weapons of 1798', illustrated talk on the uniforms and
 weapons of the United Irishmen, the Yeomanry, regular Crown
 forces and the invading French army.
SUNDAY, 31 MAY, 2.30–4.30 p.m. –
 'Who Fears to Sing of '98?', musicians sing and discuss the ballads
 of 1798, including those that celebrate the United Irishmen or
 praise the Yeomanry. Songs written both during and immediately
 after the Rebellion are performed, as well as ballads written for the
 1898 centenary.
SUNDAY, 14 JUNE, 3.00 p.m. –
 Dr Vivienne Pollock, Curator of History, Ulster Museum, 'Women
 of '98 – Women in Late 18th-Century Ireland', illustrated talk on
 the everyday lives of Irishwomen at the time of the Rebellion.
SUNDAY, 21 JUNE, 3.00 p.m. –
 Professor Tom Bartlett, University College Dublin, 'Women of '98
 – Women's Testimonies in the 1798 Court Martials', talk tracing the
 role of women in 1798 from surviving court martial records.
SUNDAY, 28 JUNE, 3.00 p.m. –
 Horace Reid, local historian, 'The Betsy Gray Legend', illustrated
 talk examining the evidence and the myths surrounding the partici-
 pation and death of Betsy Gray during the Battle of Ballynahinch.
SUNDAY, 9 AUG., 3.00 p.m. –
 Jane Leonard, Exhibition Outreach Officer, Ulster Museum, and
 Philip Anderson, professional banner artist, 'Banner Painting in
 Ulster since 1798', illustrated talk on banners and banner painting.
MONDAY, 10 AUG., from 2.00 p.m. –
 'Painting Banners', children over eight years of age can try their
 hand at painting United Irish, Yeomanry and French flags, with the
 help of professional banner artist Philip Anderson.
TUESDAY 11 AUG., from 2.00 p.m. –
 'Painting Banners', another chance for children to try their hand at
 flag painting, helped by Philip Anderson.

5

The Bicentenary Commemorations
in the South

Commemorative stamps issued by An Post, 1998

IN THE SOUTH, commemorative programmes, locally and nationally, were greatly assisted by the Government's Commemoration Committee. At Government Buildings on Tuesday, 20 January 1998, An Taoiseach, Mr Bertie Ahern TD, made the following speech to open the Government's Programme of Commemorations for the Bicentenary of 1798. This speech and the one following by Minister Seamus Brennan are quoted extensively here, as they are important indicators of the Government's attitudes to the '98 period and its commemoration, and also to the political situation in the north:

> It is my great honour to launch the Government's Programme to commemorate the 1798 Rebellion. The event touches and belongs to all traditions on this island, as well as to many of the Irish communities overseas.
>
> It is the Government's intention to treat the Commemoration with sensitivity, with due regard to historical fact, and to draw from it lessons, encouragement and inspiration for our work today of establishing lasting peace and reconciliation by agreement on this island.
>
> We are commemorating a number of things this year.
>
> We are first of all commemorating the dawn of the democratic age in Ireland, where people sought equal civil rights, parliamentary reform and religious emancipation, and, in the context of their refusal, the right to national independence.
>
> Secondly, we are commemorating the most sustained effort in Irish history, to reconcile and unite what were then three communities with different religious beliefs and ethnic backgrounds. The initiative for this came from humane and enlightened people of all traditions. This ideal has passed into history in the immortal words of Wolfe Tone. The means to independence was 'to unite the whole people of Ireland; to abolish the memory of all past dissensions and to substitute the common name of Irishmen in place of the denominations of Protestant, Catholic and Dissenter'.
>
> The United Irishmen recognised, unlike many of their successors, that an independent united Ireland crucially depended on

establishing unity and healing the distrust between the main traditions. Tone's generation realised that the idea of political independence based on a narrow Protestant ascendancy was not feasible. But he and his contemporaries who knew the North well would have been equally clear that the independence of the entire island could not be achieved solely by and for the community that was in a large numerical majority, particularly in the South, namely the Catholics. In that regard, we have been slow in learning the lessons of Irish history. In this Commemoration, we will be giving emphasis to the way in which people of different traditions worked together for their country as a whole.

Thirdly, we commemorate the suffering and the sacrifices made by the thousands of people, who died or were wounded, or who were transported, in the course of, or in the aftermath of, the Rebellion. Many of them were caught up in an impossible position, forced to defend themselves against tyranny and oppression. But there were also many honest and honourable Loyalist victims who were civilians caught up in the Rebellion in Wexford and elsewhere. We should acknowledge and remember their sufferings as well.

Fourthly, we commemorate the events of the rebellion in their own locality, in Wexford, in Carlow, in Wicklow and the South-East, in Dublin, in Kildare and Meath; in Mayo and Longford; in Antrim and Down, recognising that there were also manifestations in most other counties of Ireland.

Fifthly, we commemorate the political alliances, especially with revolutionary France, which tried to give some assistance, but also with radicals and United Men in Scotland and England. Today, we are partners in the European Union with France, Germany, Spain and other countries with which we have historic ties, as well as with Britain, in a way that does not conflict with any selfish strategic or economic interest of the neighbouring island. We should also remember that at all times in the history of the last two centuries the Irish people had friends across the water, not just oppressors. 1798 also marked with Jemmy Hope, the weaver from the Liberties and his friends and contemporaries, the beginnings of political consciousness among the working people of Dublin.

Women also played an important role in 1798. One thinks, for example, of Mary-Ann McCracken, sister of Henry Joy, one of the first political prisoners in Kilmainham. She was also a close friend of Thomas Russell. We also think of Matilda Tone, who did so much to revive the memory of Wolfe Tone in the following half century.

Sixthly, we commemorate the subsequent contribution made by Irish participants in the building of new countries, notably the United States and Australia. The ideals of the United Irishmen were carried by people like Thomas Addis Emmet and William Sampson to the United States, people who helped to establish in these countries real civil and religious liberty. We honour likewise the contribution of Michael Dwyer and his generation, and indeed a subsequent generation exiled half a century later in 1848, to the creation of the modern Australia that we see today with its strong egalitarian ethos. Nor should we overlook the important role played by the Irish in Newfoundland where the United Irishmen staged a rising in 1800.

To sum up, we honour people and their ideals. We must recognise, however, that the events of 1798 were also tragic in their human and political consequences. Thousands died, often horribly. There were atrocities on all sides. The effect of the Rebellion and the interpretation put on it by the victors served to estrange North and South, which began to go their separate ways, and that has left a legacy that has not yet healed.

The Rebellion was used as a reason to dispense with whatever limited political autonomy Ireland possessed with its own Parliament, so that it should not over time fall into the hands of a Catholic majority, with the result that, politically speaking, Ireland was emasculated for over a century. No one can draw the lesson from 1798 that the modern equivalent of the pike is the only way forward. There may have been very much less choice available in the circumstances of that time. Today, the demand for reform and equality cannot be suppressed. The way is open to negotiate a political settlement peacefully and on a footing of equality and under the auspices not only of the British Government but of a sovereign Irish Government, that can trace its political lineage back to 1798, when the first Republics in Wexford and Connacht were declared. But we should also acknowledge that there were many of the Unionist and even the present-day Orange tradition, whose ancestors were members of the United Irishmen.

Apart from its serious political significance, there is also a straightforward cultural dimension that will be reflected in the

programme. People should enjoy the year, take part in the festivities, and learn more about our past. I would like to congratulate all
the people who have been active around the country in preparing
for the year. We all hope that in the right spirit the
Commemoration can be of lasting benefit to all the people of the
island. Understandably, the best way of all to crown the bicentenary and to fulfil some of the ideals of the United Irishmen would
be to reach a new lasting and peaceful end to the conflict that has
afflicted Northern Ireland in particular over the past 30 years.

Miles Byrne of Wexford wrote in his memoirs long afterwards,
'The United Irishmen laboured for nothing but civil and religious
liberty for Irishmen of all persuasions and for the independence of
their country.'

All the people of Ireland today still share at least some of those
ideals.

The speech by the Minister of State, Seamus Brennan TD, Chairperson of the Government's 1798 Commemoration Committee,
was as follows. This is an indication of the extent and nature of the
Government's support of commemoration at home and abroad:

Our focus has been very much on partnership initiatives, especially with local communities. I am anxious that the 1798
Commemoration should not be the exclusive preserve of historians
and specialists, but that ownership of it should be claimed by all
the Irish people. I am delighted, therefore, that we have been able
to, and will endeavour to continue to, support initiatives stemming
from within the counties heavily involved in 1798 – notably
Wicklow, Dublin, Wexford, Longford, Carlow, Kildare, Kilkenny,
Mayo, Sligo, Meath, Cork, Donegal, Antrim and Down.

Not surprisingly perhaps, Co. Wexford has been forging ahead
in preparing for the bicentenary and I am very pleased to have been
able to work closely with Comóradh '98 in establishing the
National 1798 Centre. This is appropriately located under the
shadow of Vinegar Hill at Enniscorthy, the epicentre of the rebellion, and among the highlights of the year will be its opening in the
Spring.

But while Wexford is important, it is not the whole story of '98.
As recent research is demonstrating, Dublin had a crucial role to
play. I am delighted to have the opportunity to work with the

Office of Public Works, in association with the Department of Arts, Heritage, Gaeltacht and the Islands, and the National Museum at Collins Barracks in developing a dignified and sensitive memorial at Croppies' Acre.

It was in Collins Barracks that Wolfe Tone died in 1798. The Barracks is fronted by Croppies' Acre where those executed in 1798 and 1803 were summarily buried. It is important that those who died are remembered in a dignified and appropriate fashion. We have already collaborated very successfully with the OPW on the National Famine Memorial at Croagh Patrick in County Mayo, and we look forward to having this major Dublin memorial to 1798 in place during the year.

I am also pleased that my Committee has made funding available to Kevin Dawson of RTÉ to assist with the production costs of three one-hour documentaries on 1798, scheduled to be aired in the Spring. I am sure that these programmes, which emphasise the local, national and international context of the Rebellion, will greatly assist in generating interest in 1798.

We must also take account of the international perspective of the United Irishmen – to link Bunker Hill, the Bastille and Boolavogue, to stress the enduring links which '98 forged with America, France, Australia, and Newfoundland. 1798 was not just a series of minor skirmishes, but part of an international movement, indelibly linking Ireland to what was happening elsewhere in the Atlantic world. It was Ireland's first modern Revolution, which was profoundly inspired by the American and French Revolutions.

It is to mark that link that the Tour de France is coming to Ireland this year, and we welcome it as a major public event of the commemoration – both because of the French connection with the rebellion, and because it gives thousands, if not millions of ordinary people an opportunity to participate in a thrilling public spectacle.

Continuing our international theme, there will be lecture tours in America and Australia, to which many hundreds of United Irishmen were transported. A similar international focus is evident in the staging of Mozart's great Requiem. This will be performed by a talented group of singers and musicians drawn from North and South and will be performed in Wexford, Dublin and Belfast.

Mention of Belfast brings me to consider the Northern dimension to 1798. It would be wrong to think that the United Irishmen belong exclusively to our present-day Nationalist tradition. They belong, equally to the beginnings of an Irish democratic tradition, which can be shared by all, including Unionists. The Presbyterian tradition, with its enlightened emphasis on justice, equality, liberty and tolerance, was absolutely pivotal to the United Irish movement.

The Presbyterian United Irish leaders of the North understood the need for equality and inclusion. They and their generosity of spirit remain to this day an honour to the tradition from which they came. In recognition of the Ulster dimension and in a positive spirit of co-operation, my Committee has funded the major international conference '1798: A Bicentenary Perspective', which appropriately begins in Belfast and finishes in Dublin. We are also supporting the 1798 exhibition at the Linen Hall Library in Belfast, which has strong historical links with the United Irishmen. Part of this same initiative will involve the creation of an education pack for distribution to schools, both North and South. These initiatives reflect the close consultation we have undertaken with those involved in commemoration activities in Northern Ireland, where, I am happy to see, a very lively interest is being shown in 1798.

In a similar spirit, the Irish and British Governments have co-funded a three year commemoration scholarship, based at the Institute of Irish Studies in Liverpool University, which explores the influence of the United Irishmen on British radicalism in the 1790s and I am glad that the holder of that Scholarship, Gillian O'Brien is with us here today.

There will also be two ecumenical services – at St Patrick's Cathedral, Dublin, and at St Iberius Church in Wexford. These services will honour all those who died in 1798. We do not intend to gloss over the difficult issues of 1798 – like sectarianism or the use of violence. We want to confront those painful issues in a spirit of openness and honesty. We cannot walk away from our past: neither can we ignore those who differ from us in attitude or political orientation ...

... As you will see in the Information Pack, there are many other significant and interesting projects in the Programme of Commemoration, including, for example, the re-publication of Wolfe Tone's autobiography, exhaustively edited by Professor

Thomas Bartlett of UCD, the National Library and National Museum exhibition which will open in May at Collins Barracks, the Irish Theatre Archive Exhibition at Dublin Civic Museum, and the Humbert, Parnell, and Byrne/Perry Summer Schools in Mayo, Wicklow and Wexford.

We are also keen to develop fresh angles on 1798. For example, the Film Institute of Ireland, with our assistance, is presenting a major 1798 film festival on 27–28 February, during which cinematic coverage of 1798 is presented, including historic films and news coverage of earlier commemorations. We are also actively developing projects to highlight the important role of women in1798, a role which to date, has in the committee's view, received insufficient attention.

I have referred to some highlights and tried to give a flavour of the National Programme of Commemoration. But it is already clear that the ideals and events of '98 are again capturing the imagination and attention of a very wide public in all parts of Ireland. Over and above the commemorative events being sponsored or supported by our National Committee, there is a strong popular movement of local pride and activity which is, in turn, being reflected in creative initiatives in the local media. This is very much what I and the Government had hoped to see and it is indeed good to see 'the heather blazing' throughout the country.

Let me finish by emphasising once more that the United Irishmen are very much our contemporaries, in that they faced the same problems as we do but they proposed a strikingly original solution to them. Rather than seeing religious, ethnic and political diversity as a disabling problem, the United Irishmen saw these diversities as a glorious opportunity to construct a wider, more tolerant and generous vision of Irish identity. Rather than clinging to a divisive past, the United Irishmen sought to create a shared future.

It is my hope and intention that this Bicentenary commemoration will encourage us towards that imaginative inclusiveness which the United Irishmen identified as being essential to unite Protestant, Catholic and Dissenter.

Both ministerial speeches referred to the historic issues of 1798 but they also placed them in a modern political framework from the point of view of the main governing party. In this they chimed with the views of the majority of Nationalists at that moment. Government commemorations involving ministers and units of the armed forces took place, notably at Killala, Co. Mayo, 22–23 August – with French participation, as in 1798. Particularly poignant was the opening of the 'Croppies' Acre' Garden of Remembrance at Collins Barracks, Dublin. Here lay buried in an unmarked plot many of those executed in 1798. At that ceremony, the last official commemorative event in the south, An Taoiseach, Bertie Ahern, made particular reference to the involvement and sacrifice of Presbyterians and other Protestants in 1798. He said that it was imperative that Nationalists and Republicans be 'generous' in their dealings with their Protestant fellow-countrymen, in line with the United Irishmen's ideal of a 'Brotherhood of Affection'.[108]

In May 1998, An Post issued a series of commemorative stamps by leading artist Robert Ballagh. These depicted Wolfe Tone, Henry Joy McCracken, a French soldier, a heroic rebel, and 'Liberty' portraying the role of women in the struggle. With Government support, many bodies enthusiastically set about their programmes.

There wasn't much commercial exploitation of the bicentenary. However, two alcoholic drinks were produced. 'Cream of '98', an Irish cream liqueur, was 'produced in association with Comóradh '98'. Its label depicts the Battle of Oulart. '1798 Revolution Red Ale' bears on its label the United Irish harp badge with the motto 'It is new strung and shall be heard'.

Political parties and movements *per se* seemingly absented themselves from commemorative events. At Vinegar Hill on 22 January, Gerry Adams addressed a crowd of some 5,000. There was some criticism of the juxtaposition, on posters for the event, of a tribute to Gorey man Eddie O'Brien who was killed on a London bus when a bomb he was allegedly carrying exploded prematurely in 1996.

In general, commemorative programmes were organised by committees composed of local government representatives and officials (some motivated to an extent by tourism opportunities), and local historians and other enthusiasts. A major part was played by academics, in particular those connected to the Government's commemoration programme: Tom Bartlett, Kevin Whelan and Daire

Keogh, as well as Ruan O'Donnell, Breandán Mac Suibhne, David Dickson and Tommy Graham, all of whom gave unsparingly of their time in addressing audiences, in every part of the country, north and south.

EXHIBITIONS

There were two excellent major exhibitions in the south. A permanent National 1798 Visitation Centre was opened by the Taoiseach at Enniscorthy, Co. Wexford on 5 June 1998. This is housed in the former Christian Brothers' monastery at Millpark Road. It is in a very appropriate site in the heartland of the Rising in Wexford, not far from Vinegar Hill. The 'Fellowship of Freedom' exhibition, in the Collins Barracks annexe of the National Museum of Ireland, was accompanied by a lavishly illustrated book of the same name by Kevin Whelan.

On 26 May 1998, the British Ambassador Mrs Veronica Sutherland opened the exhibition 'Croppies Lie Down: Ireland in 1798' in the Long Room, Old Library, Trinity College Dublin. The Royal Irish Academy, 16 Dawson Street, Dublin held '1798 From Contemporary Sources: an exhibition' from 1 September 1998 to 8 January 1999. 'Who Fears to Speak' was put in place by the Friends of 1798 Committee from 14 to 21 August at the Branch Library, Clones, Co. Monaghan. Further smaller '98 exhibitions with local themes were held throughout Ireland (see local sections below).

CONFERENCES AND SUMMER SCHOOLS

The bicentenary spawned a number of well-attended academic conferences and events which reflected the huge scholarly interest in '98. The Glencree Centre for Reconciliation in Co. Wicklow held a seminar on 26–27 February 1798, 'From Rebellion to Reconciliation: the Women of 1798 and 1998'. The appropriateness of this venue for the seminar was pointed out in the invitation letter:

> The Glencree Centre for Reconciliation was built as a direct result
> of the 1798 Rebellion. It began its life as a British Army barracks
> and its present incarnation as a Centre for Reconciliation symbol-

ises the journey of our two nations. This symbolism and journey is represented by the opening address by Her Excellency the President of Ireland Mary McAleese and closing address by Her Excellency Veronica Sutherland the British Ambassador to Ireland.

The Royal Irish Academy Committee for the Study of Anglo-Irish Literature held a conference and symposium on '1798: Revolution, Memory, Imagination' at Academy House, Kildare Street and the National Library of Ireland, Dublin on 27–28 March 1998. This mainly dealt with relevant literary themes.

Saor-Ollscoil na hÉireann (Free University of Ireland) held a summer school on 1798 at Prussia Street, Dublin from 11 to 16 May 1798.

The major bicentenary academic event was the two-part conference in the Ulster Museum (19–20 May 1998) and Dublin Castle (21–23 May). It was sponsored by the Irish Government 1798 Commemoration Committee, the Northern Ireland Community Relations Council and Allied Irish Bank. It had the same organisers as the two-centre academic conference commemorating the bicentenary of the United Irishmen in 1991. A publication based on the papers delivered now provides a further major collection on the United Irishmen.[109]

The Society for the Study of Nineteenth Century Ireland held a conference at UCC, 26–28 June 1998, with the theme '1798, 1848, 1898: Revolution, Revival and Commemoration'.

Naturally, Ireland's many weekend and summer schools took their theme from '98, beginning with the Merriman, held at Westport on the weekend of 30 January–1 February. The annual Byrne/Perry Summer School was held at the Masonic Hall, Gorey, 26–28 June 1998, with the theme 'The 1798 Rebellion and Its Aftermath'. Directed by Daire Keogh, this naturally was a showpiece for his colleagues on the '98 lecture circuit. The Parnell Summer School at Avondale, 9–18 August, addressed 'The Republic'. The annual Humbert School in Ballina in August had more than usual appropriateness that year.

LOCAL COMMEMORATIONS

Although Dublin has been described as 'the dog that didn't bark' due to its failure to rise in 1798, the bicentenary was well marked. The Dublin 1798 Commemoration Committee set up a major lecture programme, from November 1997 to May 1998, involving prominent '98 historians Tom Bartlett, Brian Cleary, Ruan O'Donnell, Kevin Whelan, Daire Keogh, Tommy Graham, Breandán Mac Suibhne, and Mary Cullen. These were to be described affectionately, later in the commemoration year, as 'the usual suspects', so widespread was their speaking circuit throughout the country. Each in turn gave a lecture at the following venues in and around the capital: Kilmainham Gaol; Central Library, ILAC Centre; and the libraries at Rathmines, Rathbeale, Swords, Donaghmede, Raheny, Ballymun, Deansgrange, Blanchardstown, Ballyfermot, Clondalkin, Castletymon, Ballyroan and the County Library at Tallaght. Talks in South Dublin Council area were accompanied by a '1798 in South Dublin Exhibition'. The Dublin committee also produced an excellent souvenir programme containing a potted history of the United Irishmen by its secretary, Tommy Graham, and a reprint of the long-lost radical United Irish pamphlet *The Union Doctrine or Poor Man's Cathechism*.

Fingal had the following programme of events (Comóradh '98 Fine Gall/Fingal '98).

12 APRIL –
- 11.30 a.m. – Fingal Brigade Old IRA. Mass in Ballyboughal, followed by parade to '98 monument at Drishogue Lane.
  Prominent speakers included Sean Ryan, Philip Jenkinson, Trevor Sargent, Peadar Bates and Paddy Weston.
- 1.00 p.m. – Traditional session and sing-song in O'Connor's, Ballyboughal.
- 8.00–11.00 p.m. – Ceili in St Patrick's Hall, Ballyboughal.

16 MAY – Seminar exploring the importance of 1798 from a local, regional and national perspective, Ardgillan Castle.

23 MAY –
- 12.00 noon – Re-enactment of mailcoach hijacking by Fingal Pikemen at Ballough/Man O'War.
- 2.00 p.m. – Fingal '98 Committee and Fingal Pikemen march

to Curragha for unveiling of Paid O'Donoghue Memorial, followed by *ceol & craic*.

24 MAY – 2.00 p.m. Traditional house session to commemorate the siege of Westpalstown Barracks by local Fingal insurgents at MacPhilibins of Westpalstown.

11–12 JULY – Pageant commemorating the last stand of Wexfordmen at Drishogue, pipe bands, mummers, pikemen and redcoats. Everyone welcome.

12 JULY – 9.00 p.m. Ceili in St Patrick's Hall, Ballyboughal.

Other events included a play on the life and times of Molly Weston by Rush Dramatic Society, and *The Stag of the Naul*, adapted by Tommy Monaghan.

There were many other local commemoration committees throughout the 26 counties, particularly in areas directly involved in 1798. By far the largest of the local commemorative programmes in the south was that of Comóradh '98, centred in Wexford, as befitted the county most heavily involved in 1798. In all the work of Comóradh, Bernard Browne, Director of the 1798 Centre at Enniscorthy, played a pivotal role. Among the major events in the Wexford calendar was the session of the Wexford Senate at Johnstown Castle on 31 June 1998, to commemorate the body set up during the Rising of 1798. The 'Senators' were 350 nominees from all over the Irish diaspora, each sponsored to the tune of £2,000. President Mary McAleese was on hand to open officially the re-creation of the cottage of Fr Murphy at Boolavogue on 13 April.

Programme of Comóradh '98

31 DECEMBER 1997 –
Official Opening Ceremony, carrying torches to Vinegar Hill.

1 JANUARY 1998 –
Ceremonial Flag Raising, Market Square, Enniscorthy.

2 JANUARY –
- Opening Concert, Concert Hall, Enniscorthy.
- Commemorative Concert, National Concert Hall, Dublin.

LATE JAN.–DEC. –
Exhibition on 1798, National Library, Dublin.

7 FEBRUARY –
Seminar, Ferrycarrig Hotel, Wexford.

3–9 MARCH – The Show – *Who Fears To Speak?*, Dún Mhuire, Wexford.

7 APRIL – Mozart *Requiem* '98 (commemorating all the dead of '98, involving the Ulster Orchestra and choirs from the north and south-east and France), Rowe Street Church, Wexford Town.

8 APRIL –
Mozart *Requiem* '98, National Concert Hall, Dublin.

13 APRIL –
Official Opening of the Fr John Murphy Centre, Boolavogue (a reconstruction of his house).

15–19 APRIL –
Slógadh '98 youth festival of Irish music, song, dance and drama with a '98 theme.

24–25 APRIL –
Kilkenny Archaeological Society Seminar (with a '98 theme), Rothe House, Kilkenny.

26 APRIL –
Unveiling of 1798 module on Slieve Coillte, J.F. Kennedy Park, New Ross.

1 MAY –
Unveiling of Harvey/Colclough Memorial, Kilmore Quay, Co. Wexford.

9 MAY –
Federation of Local History Societies, Spring Seminar, Talbot Hotel, Wexford.

10 MAY–18 JULY –
Portable Art '98 (contemporary Irish art on the '98 theme), The Watch House Gallery, Enniscorthy.

13 MAY –
Castledockrell Commemoration, Enniscorthy.

19–23 MAY –
International Academic Conference on 1798, Ulster Museum (19–20 May) and Dublin Castle (20–23 May).

22–24 MAY –
Boolavogue '98 Weekend, Boolavogue, Enniscorthy.[110]

23 MAY –
Concert to commemorate the original date of the Rising, in

Smithfield, Dublin City Centre.

24 MAY –
Oulart Commemoration, Oulart, Co. Wexford.[111]

30 MAY –
Wexford Senate Weekend, Johnstown Castle, Wexford.

30 MAY –
Three Rocks Commemoration, Barntown, near Wexford.

31 MAY – Commemoration at Carrigbyrne Hill, Carrigbyrne, Co.
Wexford.

1 JUNE –
Commemoration of the Battle of Newtownbarry, Bunclody.

4 JUNE –
Pageant entitled 'The Gathering of the Bantry Men' at
Monksgrange, Kilanne, Co. Wexford.

5 JUNE –
Official opening by An Taoiseach, Bertie Ahern TD, of the National
1798 Visitor Centre, Enniscorthy, Co. Wexford. Pageant representing the Battle of New Ross, New Ross, Co. Wexford.

6 JUNE –
Memorial wreath-laying, Scullabogue, Co. Wexford.

7 JUNE –
Piercetown/Murrintown Commemoration, Rathaspeck/Johnstown
Castle near Wexford.

14 JUNE –
National Ecumenical Service, St Patrick's Cathedral, Dublin.

15 JUNE –
Lacken Hill Pageant, near New Ross, Co. Wexford.

19–20 JUNE –
Commemoration of the Battle of Goff's Bridge, Foulksmills, Co.
Wexford.

21 JUNE –
Vinegar Hill Day (the major outdoor event of the Commemorative
year), Enniscorthy, Co. Wexford.

21 JUNE –
Unveiling of memorial at Duncormick, Co. Wexford.

22 JUNE –
Sponsored charity walk of 52 miles retracing the epic march of Fr
John Murphy following Vinegar Hill, from Sleedagh to Tomduff,
Co. Wexford.

24–26 JUNE –
Byrne/Perry Summer School, Gorey, Co. Wexford (see section on
summer schools).

26 JUNE –
Ballindaggin Commemoration, Enniscorthy.

28 JUNE –
Bagenal Harvey Flotilla to commemorate his retreat from Wexford
Harbour to the Saltee Islands.

29 JUNE –5 July –
Tullow Commemoration, Co. Carlow (where Fr John Murphy was
executed).

13–20 JULY –
Exhibition of '98 Memorabilia and artefacts, Wexford.

14 JULY –
Bastille Day Ball, Teeling Centre, Colloney, Co. Sligo.

19 JULY –
St Mullins '98 Commemoration, St Mullins, Co. Carlow.

26 JULY –
Killane Commemoration, Enniscorthy.

19–23 AUG. –
General Humbert Summer School, Ballina/Killala/Lacken, Co.
Mayo.

19–29 AUG. –
Insurrection '98 (historical documentary drama by Nicholas
Furlong), Dún Mhuire, Wexford.

22–29 AUG. –
Killala Festival (a week of '98 events with a French connection), Co.
Mayo.

23 AUG –
1798 Humbert Commemoration, Enniscoe, Lahardane,
Crossmolina, Co. Mayo.

29 AUG –5 Sept. –
Ballinamuck '98 Festival, Co. Longford.

12 SEPT. –
Re-enactment of the Battle of Carrignagat, Collooney, Co. Sligo.

24 OCT. –
Film Festival – international films based on the theme of 'Liberty,
Equality and Fraternity', Wexford Film Club, Wexford Arts Centre.

22–26 OCT. –
Antiques Fair featuring memorabilia from the 1790s, Talbot Hotel,
Wexford.

The Bicentenary in Wicklow

Wicklow '98 Committee/Coiste Chill Mhantáin '98 had a very

extensive programme, as befitted the county where the United Irishmen held out longest due to the activities of Michael Dwyer and his close associates. Events were as follows:

1 JAN. –
> Flag-raising ceremony, unveiling of plaque to Brother Luke Cullen ('98 historian), planting of 'Tree of Freedom', Bray.

1 JAN. –
> Flag-raising ceremony, Arklow.

2 JAN. –
> Launch of Wicklow '98 Committee/Coiste Chill Mhantáin '98 Programme, Powerscourt.

3 JAN. –
> Planting of 'Tree of Freedom' by Joe Jacob, Minster of State, Glendalough.

22 JAN. –
> '98 in Wicklow' – a lecture by Dr R. O'Donnell, Bray.

26 JAN. –
> Wicklow Australia Day.

9 FEB. –
> Launch of Wicklow '98 Committee/Coiste Chill Mhantáin '98 Wicklow 1798 Educational Pack, Wicklow.

15 FEB. –
> Dwyer Bicentenary Walk 1, 'Dwyer/McAllister Commemorative Walk', Glen of Imaal.

19 FEB. –
> 'Republicanism, Its Relevance in Today's Politics', a lecture by Dr John McManus, Bray.

26–27 FEB. –
> International Women's Day Conference: 'From Rebellion to Reconciliation', Glencree. Opened by President Mary McAleese; addresses by UK and US Ambassadors.

1–8 MAR. –
> 29th Arklow Music Festival – Original '98 Poem.

2 MAR. –
> 'The Byrnes of Ballymanus', Rathdrum Historical Society lecture by Dr Conor O'Brien, Rathdrum.

14–22 MAR. –
> Wicklow Heritage Centre 1798 Exhibition, Glen of Imaal.

17 MAR. –
> Dwyer Bicentenary Walk 2, 'Dwyer/McAllister Commemorative Walk', Glen of Imaal.

28 MAR. –
Wicklow Historical Society '1798 Forum', Wicklow.

APRIL –
Official Opening of Wicklow's Historic Gaol, Wicklow.

APRIL –
Commemorative Walk 1, Baltinglass.

3–5 APR. –
Junior Chamber Ireland's Spring Conference Commemorating Wicklow's 1798 Heritage, Wicklow.

6 APR. –
'Wicklow Gaol and '98', Rathdrum Historical Society lecture by Joan Kavanagh, Rathdrum.

12 APR –
Dwyer/McAllister Commemorative Road Race, Glen of Imaal.

12 APR –
Launch of the Liam Mellows Traditional Group's *Musical Tribute to '98* tape and booklet, Royal Hotel, Arklow.

18 APR –
Unveiling of plaque to Peter Burke and Thomas White, Bray.

19 APR –
Bicentenary Walk 3, 'Dwyer Surrender Walk', Glen of Imaal.

MAY –
Commemorative Walk 2, Baltinglass.

1–4 MAY –
1798 Schools' History Competition, Bray Heritage Centre.

2–4 MAY –
Tinahely '98 Weekend: ceremony to unveil plaque (2 May), fireworks and street music (3 May), march to Ballyrahan and service (4 May).

2–4 MAY –
Wicklow Heritage Centre 1798 Exhibition, Tinahely.

3 MAY –
A heritage walk around Arklow.

5–7 MAY –
Shibboleth Theatre Company, Belfast, Drama Workshops – 'A Catalyst for Reflection on the 1798 Rebellion', Wicklow.

6 MAY –
Shibboleth Theatre Company presented *The Turnout*, 'a fresh look at the 1798 Rebellion, focusing on three women whose lives and deaths illuminate the nature of this peculiar time'.

8 MAY –
Unveiling of Wicklow '98 Committee/Coiste Chill Mhantáin '98

commemorative plaque, Ballymanus.

8–10 MAY –

Roundwood & District Historical & Folklore Society Seminar.

10 MAY –

Unveiling of the Joseph Holt Memorial, Roundwood.

10–16 MAY –

'Words and Music Commemorate 1798', Bridge Tavern, Wicklow.

11 MAY –

'The Role of Women in the 1798 Rebellion' Rathdrum Historical Society lecture by Anna Kinsella.

15–17 MAY –

'98 commemorative weekend, Humewood Castle.

16 May –

The story of Michael Dwyer through drama, song and dance, 'Master of the Mountains, the Story of the Roots, the Campaign, and the Aftermath of the 1798 rebellion', Humewood Castle.

17 MAY –

Bicentenary Walk 4, 'Dwyer/McAllister Commemorative Walk', Glen of Imaal.

23 MAY –

Parade/Pageant commemoration, Roundwood.

23 MAY–1 June –

Newcastle & District '98 Féile. Parade and unveiling of 1798 commemorative stone (23 May); guided historical walk (May 24); exhibitions and lectures (23–31 May); various gatherings with Irish traditional and Breton music and crossroads dance (30 May–1 June).

23 MAY–31 AUG. –

Bray Heritage Centre 1798 Exhibition.

24 MAY –

Unveiling of Carnew Shillelagh & Coolboy Districts Comóradh '98 Memorial.

24 MAY –

Carnew Commemorative Festival.

24 MAY –

Re-dedication of Dunlavin–Tournant memorial and religious service at Tournant graveyard.

24 MAY –

Unveiling of Wicklow '98 Committee/Coiste Chill Mhantáin '98 commemorative plaque, Dunlavin.

24 MAY –

Unveiling of Wicklow '98 Committee/Coiste Chill Mhantáin '98 commemorative plaque, Baltinglass.

24 MAY –

Unveiling of Wicklow '98 Committee/Coiste Chill Mhantáin '98 commemorative plaque, Stratford.

29–31 MAY –

Byrne Clan Rally. The gathering of the Byrnes, registration, reception, Woodenbridge; welcome by the Chieftains, *ceol agus craic* (29 May); seminar, guided tour of Wicklow Gaol, celebration banquet followed by music and dancing (30 May); ecumenical service, guided bus tours of O'Byrne Country and other '98 locations (31 May).

30 MAY –

Unveiling of Wicklow '98 Committee/Coiste Chill Mhantáin '98 commemorative plaque, Newtownmountkennedy.

31 MAY –

Ballinglen Commemorative Sunday, Baltinglass.

JUNE –

Glencree Reconciliation Centre Exhibition.

JUNE –

Commemorative Walk 3, Baltinglass.

JUNE –

'Fair Hills of Ireland' – Australian Tour by '98 descendants.

1 JUNE –

Unveiling of Wicklow '98 Committee/Coiste Chill Mhantáin '98 commemorative plaque, Carnew.

1–14 JUNE –

Battle of Arklow Commemorations, Arklow.

4 JUNE –

Dedication of William Putnam McCabe Room at Bray Quinn's Hotel (Royal).

9 JUNE –

Unveiling of Wicklow '98 Committee/Coiste Chill Mhantáin '98 commemorative plaque, Arklow.

12 JUNE –

'1798 Period Costume Outdoor Feast', Glen of Imaal.

14 JUNE –

Parade and pageant, Arklow.

14 JUNE –

'1798 Bus Tour of Wicklow'.

14 JUNE –

The Glen of Imaal '98 Festival.

18 JUNE –

Unveiling of plaque to Captain Edwards, followed by 'Captain

Edwards of Oldcourt', a lecture by Eva Ó Cathaoir, Bray.

18 and 20 JUNE –

Street Pageant of Billy Byrne, Wicklow Drama Group, Wicklow.

18–21 JUNE –

The Wicklow Midsummer '98 Pageant.

JULY –

Commemorative Walk 4, Baltinglass.

5–11 JULY –

Synge Summer School, 'Theatre and History', Rathdrum.

12 JULY –

Wicklow Pike Men/Women salute Tour de France.

14 JULY –

Bastille Day, Wicklow.

19 JULY –

Unveiling of Ballymanus Gaelic Football Club Plaque to Billy Byrne, Ballymanus.

19 JULY –

Dwyer/McAllister Commemorative Bicentenary Walk 5, Glen of Imaal.

20 JULY –

Billy Byrne Anniversary Memorial Service, Ballymanus House.

27 JULY –

Unveiling of Wicklow '98 Committee/Coiste Chill Mhantáin '98 commemorative plaque, Powerscourt.

AUGUST –

Commemorative Walk 5, Baltinglass.

1 AUG. –

Unveiling of plaque to United Irishmen (including Kennedy, Ledwidge and Nugent) and the Bray Yeomanry, Bray Courthouse.

2 AUG. –

Glendalough–Seven Churches Guided '98 Walk with Dr Ruan O'Donnell.

2 AUG. –

Unveiling of Wicklow '98 Committee/Choiste Chill Mhantáin '98 commemorative plaque, Glendalough.

8 AUG. –

West Wicklow Historical Society Seminar, Baltinglass.

9–16 AUG. –

Parnell Summer School – 'The Republic', Rathdrum.

9 AUG. –

Opening of 1798 Memorial Park, Glenmalure.

10–16 AUG. –
Glenmalure 1798–1998 Bicentenary Festival Week – parade, historical walks, music, dance, lectures, exhibition of historical data, 1798 arts exhibition.

15 AUG. 1798 –
Historical Tour hosted by Greenan Farm – Museums & Maze and Glenmalure Lodge.

15 AUG. –
Opening of 1798 Commemorative Park, Rathdrum.

21–23 AUG. –
'Reconciling Conflicting Views of History: 1798 in the context of Peace Building', Glencree Centre Summer School.

24 AUG. –
Unveiling of Wicklow '98 Committee/Coiste Chill Mhantáin '98 commemorative plaque, Wicklow.

31 AUG. –
Closing of 1798 exhibition, Bray.

4 SEPT. –
Period Costume Garden Party, Bray.

5 SEPT. –
Unveiling of Wicklow '98 Committee/Coiste Chill Mhantáin '98 commemorative plaque, Blessington.

6 SEPT. –
Excursion to Michael Dwyer Cottage with talk by Dr Ruan O'Donnell, Derrynamuck.

18 SEPT. –
'98 Commemorative Ball, Bray.

19 SEPT. –
Unveiling of Aughrim District Comóradh '98 Memorial.

19 SEPT. –
Unveiling of Wicklow '98 Committee/Coiste Chill Mhantáin '98 commemorative plaque, Aughrim.

20 SEPT. –
Dwyer/McAllister Commemorative Bicentenary Walk 6, Glen of Imaal.

1 OCT. –
Unveiling of Wicklow '98 Committee/Coiste Chill Mhantáin '98 commemorative plaque, Delgany.

16 OCT. –
Unveiling of Wicklow '98 Committee/Coiste Chill Mhantáin '98 commemorative plaque, Rathdrum.

30 OCT. –
   Wicklow Junior Chamber '98 Commemorative Period Masquerade
   Ball, Wicklow.
NOVEMBER –
   '98 Film Festival, Wicklow.
10 NOV. –
   'Joseph Holt', a lecture by Dr Ruan O'Donnell, Bray.
DECEMBER –
   Unveiling of Wicklow '98 Committee/Coiste Chill Mhantáin '98
   commemorative plaque, Annacurra.
14 DEC. –
   Unveiling of Wicklow '98 Committee/Coiste Chill Mhantáin '98
   commemorative plaque, Humewood.
14 DEC. –
   'Michael Dwyer', a lecture by Dr Ruan O'Donnell, Bray.
31 DEC. –
   Lowering of the Flag, Last Post, etc., Bray.
31 DEC. –
   Launch of Book of Memorial Photos of '98, Arklow.

An accompanying booklet, 'Wicklow Commemorating 1798–
1998', was published.

On 8 August 1998, West Wicklow Historical Society held a one-
day symposium at Baltinglass on the theme 'West Wicklow in
1798: Towards a Balanced View', with prominent speakers including Liam Chambers, Daire Keogh, Ruan O'Donnell and Kevin
Whelan. Also, there is a permanent exhibition on '98 in the county on the ground floor of Wicklow's Historic Gaol in Wicklow
town.

Bray, Co. Wicklow had an extensive programme of events (there
is some duplication here of events listed in the Wicklow programme above).

1 JAN. –
   Flag-raising and unveiling of plaque to Brother Luke Cullen (histo-
   rian) at Bray Heritage Centre; planting of Tree of Freedom at
   Sidmonton Road, Bray (pipers).
22 JAN. –
   ''98 in Wicklow', lecture by Dr Ruan O'Donnell, PRO of the
   Wicklow 1798 Committee and the secretary of the Irish Centre for
   Australian Studies.

19 FEB. –

'Republicanism, Its Relevance in Today's Politics', a lecture in the Esplanade Hotel by Dr John McManus, a well-known doctor in the town of Bray and also very well known in political circles, and a member of Bray Urban District Council.

19 MAR. –

'98 in Dublin' by Tommy Graham, Esplanade Hotel, Bray.

18 APR. –

Unveiling of plaque to Peter Burke and Thomas White, executed on Bray Sea Commons in 1798. The plaque at the Harbour Bar is sponsored by Wicklow County Council.

1–14 MAY –

'98 schools history competition.

10 MAY –

Unveiling of a memorial to Joseph Holt, at Mullinaveigue, Roundwood.

23 MAY –

Opening of '98 exhibition in the Heritage Centre.

4 JUNE –

Dedication of William Putnam McCabe Room at Quin's Hotel (now the Royal Hotel). McCabe originally came from Belfast. He paid several visits to the area in late 1797 and in early 1798 became acquainted with Michael Dwyer.

1 JUNE –

Unveiling of plaque to Captain Edwards in Christchurch, Church Road, Bray, followed by a lecture on Captain Edwards of Oldcourt by Eva Ó Cathaoir. Sponsored by Bray Urban District Council.

14 JUNE –

'98 bus tour of Co. Wicklow.

1 AUG. –

Unveiling of plaque to United Irishmen (including Ledwidge, Kennedy and Nugent) and the Bray Yeomanry.

30 AUG. –

Official closing of 1798 exhibition in the Heritage Centre.

4 SEPT. –

Period costume garden party hosted by Frank and Mary Doyle in the garden of their home on Church Road, Bray.

23 OCT. –

The official '98 Commemorative Ball (Bray) – in period costume, Summerhill Hotel, Enniskerry.

10 NOV. –

'Joseph Holt', a lecture by Dr Ruan O'Donnell in the Royal Hotel.

14 DEC. –

'Michael Dwyer', a lecture by Dr Ruan O'Donnell in the Royal Hotel.

31 DEC. –

Lowering of the Flag and the 'Last Post' at the Heritage Centre.

The Bicentenary elsewhere in the south

CARLOW

Carlow Bicentenary 1798 Commemoration Committee's schedule of events included, in Carlow town, a Spring Lecture Series from 5 February to 5 March, a '98 Seminar on 14 March, an annual parade to Croppies' Grave, and the Éigse festival, 4–14 June (including many events not specific to '98 but with a re-enactment of the 1798 Battle of Carlow at Potato Market). The '98 Welcome Home Week included tours to areas of '98 relevance and the unveiling of a memorial at Potato Market. An exhibition of '98 memorabilia was held in Carlow Museum–Town Hall from January to December 1998.

Commemorations of events of '98 throughout County Carlow were held as close as possible to the dates on which they had happened in 1798, at Muinebheag/Bagenalstown, Clonegal-Kildavin, Myshall, Tomduff Campfield, Hacketstown, Tullow (where there is a Fr Murphy monument), Kilcumney, Leighlin Bridge, Rathvilly, St Mullins, Clonmore, and the Royal Oak Inn. A souvenir brochure was produced by Carlow Bicentenary 1798 Commemoration Committee.

CASTLECOMER

'Castlecomer Remembers 1798' was the title of a two-day commemoration of the battle in that Co. Kilkenny town in 1798. Prominent speakers at a seminar run by Fassadinin Historical Society included Daire Keogh, Anna Kinsella, Patrick Comerford, and Nicholas Furlong. Other events included an ecumenical service, a bus tour and a concert.

DUNGARVAN

Dungarvan, Co. Waterford was the scene of a commemorative weekend from 17 to 21 June 1998 organised by Dungarvan Museum Society. This included a lecture by Daire Keogh, a symposium on Dungarvan and Waterford in 1798 with local historians, a commemoration of Edmund Power at the Old Market House and 1798 Monument in the Park and an accompanying 1798 exhibition in Dungarvan Museum.

Ballina, August 1998
French and Irish officers at the Humbert commemorations

KILLALA AND BALLINA

On 22–29 August 1998, these Co. Mayo towns saw extensive commemorative programmes involving the local community and the Irish and French Governments. On Sunday 23 August, in emulation of Humbert's landing at Kilcummin, near Killala, a French force came ashore from a naval squadron and a commemoration ceremony was held. A further military commemoration was later held at the '98 memorial in Killala with Irish and French units and dignitaries in attendance. An Taoiseach, Bertie Ahern, stressed Ireland's links then and now with France. A large number of citizens of the French town of Chauvé in Brittany were on hand for a twinning day with Killala, which took place on the Monday, bringing to a close a long weekend of historical and cultural festivities. A commemorative programme, Killala Remembering 1798, priced £2, was produced for the occasion.

COLLOONEY

In Collooney, Co. Sligo, the Collooney Commemoration Committee organised a major programme largely centred on Markree Castle, the ancestral home of the Cooper family. Also a focus point was the centenary memorial to the Co. Antrim United Irishman, Bartholomew Teeling, who distinguished himself in the fighting around Collooney. Participants were mainly local, though there was a contingent from France. The extensive programme, which ran from April to September 1998, was made up of historical and cultural events with an Irish and French emphasis. A highlight was the re-enactment of the Battle of Carrignagat, on 12 and 13 September, in which Humbert defeated forces under the command of Colonel Vereker. An exhibition and a sculpted mosaic constitute a permanent '98 memorial in the area. A video of the programme was produced. Also, there were many one-off events elsewhere in the area.

BALLINAMUCK

As befits the area where the final battle of 1798 took place, Ballinamuck, Co. Longford had a relatively extensive programme of events particularly during the week of the battle from 28 August to 5 September 1998. An excellent accompanying book, *Ballinamuck Bicentenary 1798–1998*, edited by Padraig Rehill, was published by the energetic Ballinamuck Bicentenary Committee. This gives a comprehensive history of Ballinamuck in 1798 but also includes information and illustrations pertaining to commemorations in

1898, 1908, 1928, 1938, 1948 and 1983. The centrepiece of the commemorations was the memorial to the battle erected in 1928 (see the account of its dedication in Chapter 3). The programme was as follows:

- re-enactment of the battle
- battlefield trail
- history lectures by eminent historians
- historical tour of County Longford.

Additional non-historical events were included in the 1998 programme.

BACK LANE

The last major commemorative event in the south in 1998 was held on 5 December at the Taylors' Hall, Back Lane, Dublin, opposite Christ Church. Here a re-enactment of the so-called 'Back Lane Parliament', a gathering of Catholic delegates in the 1790s, was held at its original venue. It was attended by representatives of commemorative bodies from every county in Ireland. The following day, the Sheares brothers, John and Henry, barristers and United Irish leaders, were commemorated at St Michan's Church, where they are buried in the vault. A plaque to the brothers was unveiled by the Hon. Justices Susan Denham and Donal Barrington of the Supreme Court, followed by Sunday Service.

International '98 bicentenary events

1998 was also a year of commemoration in the many parts of the world where the Irish diaspora has settled. Academic conferences were held outside Ireland to which many Irish speakers were invited, particularly in Britain, the USA and Australia. An international academic conference on 1798 was held on 30 March–1 April 1998 at Notre Dame University, Indiana. The annual symposium of the American Conference for Irish Studies, at Fort Lauderdale, Florida, 15–19 April 1998, had the theme 'Ireland in 1798 and 1848'.

Colingwood College, University of Durham, hosted the 11th Conference of Irish Historians in Britain, 3–5 April 1998,

'Memory and Commemoration in Irish History'. This included a session on 1798. The Pontifical Irish College, Rome devoted its May Lecture Series to '98 with Tom Bartlett, Minister Seamus Brennan, Daire Keogh and Kevin Whelan on the panel. In March 1998, a symposium on 1798 was held at Magdalen College, Cambridge. On Saturday, 12 September the British Association for Irish Studies, in association with Ruskin College, Oxford and *History Ireland*, held a bicentenary symposium at the college on Irish revolutionaries and British radicals. At the University of Luton a conference titled 'Ireland's Year of Liberty' was held on 24–25 July. The International Social Sciences Institute at Edinburgh University held a conference on 'Commemorating Ireland: History, Politics, Culture – a Comparative Approach', 11–12 September 1998. Naturally, '98 and its commemoration was a major conference theme.

At the university in Melbourne, Australia, an academic conference was held, 26–30 September, on the theme of Ireland in the 1790s. Also in September, President McAleese unveiled arguably the largest monument in the world to the United Irishmen, at Sydney.[112]

France was also involved in the commemorative process, with French Government events there and in Ireland. Particularly moving was the ceremony at Montmartre Cemetery, Paris, on 8 March, where the remarkable émigré, Miles Byrne, lies buried. A eulogy was delivered by Pat Power to the United Irishman, participant in Emmet's rising, Chef de Bataillon of the 56th Regiment and Chevalier of the Legion of Honour. At Brest in Brittany from 4 to 6 June 1998, 'Colloque International: 1796–1798: les Années des Francais en Irlande' was held alongside an official French Government Commemoration involving ministers, the army and navy.

THEATRE

Undoubtedly the north was better served for '98 productions during the bicentenary. As part of the Belfast Festival at Queen's, on 18–22 November 1997 in St Kevin's Hall, North Queen Street, Dock Ward Community Theatre produced *Rebellion: the Henry Joy*

McCracken Story. This was devised and written by Ken Bourke and the company, and directed by Paddy McCooey, with original music by Mark Dougherty. John Gray's adaptation of the Rev. James Porter's *Billy Bluff and Squire Firebrand* was performed at many venues throughout the north in 1997 and 1998.

There were a number of performances during the bicentenary year by Ulster musicians Jane Cassidy and Maurice Leyden and company of their musical–theatrical show *Mary Ann*. This tells the story of '98 through the life of Mary Ann McCracken (1770–1866), whose brother Henry Joy and Thomas Russell, the man she loved, were executed for their revolutionary activities.

The organisation History Through Drama, which has worked in Ireland and abroad, devised an educational package to include primary school pupils in the commemoration of the 1798 rising through drama. Resultant performances were staged at venues in a number of district council areas in the north. *The Boul Proota Diggers* was performed at several venues (see lists of council events above) by four Co. Antrim performers: Liz Weir, Willie Drennan, Bob Speares and Billy Teare.

In February and March 1998, Centre Stage mounted a revival of Jack Loudan's 1943 play *Henry Joy McCracken*, produced by Roma Tomelty and directed by Colin Carnegie, at a number of main Ulster venues and the Hawk's Well Theatre, Sligo. The play had previously been produced in Belfast's Group Theatre in 1948. Gary Mitchell's new play *Tearing the Loom*, set in 1798, appeared at Belfast's Lyric Theatre, 17 March–4 April 1998. Directed by David Grant, it focused on two Co. Armagh weaver families, the Moores and the Hamills, torn apart by the conflict between the United Irishmen and the Orange Order. Shibboleth Theatre Group mounted a new production of *The Turnout* at many venues, north and south, during May and June.

As part of the Down commemorative programme, the Down County Museum and the Hearts of Down 1998 Society collaborated in the staging of Philip Orr's *The Last Journey of Thomas Russell* at the museum (see Down programme).

Perhaps the crowning theatrical event of the bicentenary year was the joint production by the Tinderbox and Field Day Theatre

Companies of *Northern Star*. Written by the late Stewart Parker and directed by Stephen Rea, it was a Belfast Festival at Queen's co-production, staged 8–11 November 1998. *Northern Star* tells the story of Henry Joy McCracken and '98. It was staged in the very appropriate and evocative setting of the First Presbyterian Church, Rosemary Street, Belfast. In April and May 1998, the Irish Theatre Archive, 69 Middle Abbey Street, Dublin, held a retrospective exhibition, 'Rebellion! Theatre and 1798' at the Dublin Civic Museum, South William Street. As well as looking at the impact of '98 on Irish theatre, this provided a link with past commemoration.

TELEVISION

The bicentenary was something of a media event, not least in the sense that the major networks produced their own series, which could be viewed both north and south. In each case these were happy collaborations between programme-makers and the most prominent historians of the '98 era. Each made extensive use of narrative backed with location film, contemporary accounts, documentary evidence, artwork and comment by historians. BBC 1 Northern Ireland broadcast *The Patriot's Fate* in two episodes. This was produced and directed by Moore Sinnerton for his own company. Chistera Productions. The writer was historian Jonathan Bardon and it was presented by Brian Keenan, former Lebanon hostage. Part 1 (60 minutes), 'A Cordial Union', relayed on 18 February, looked at the background to the Rising. Part 2 (50 minutes): 'Not Quite Philadelphia', broadcast on 25 February, looked at the course of the various phases of the Rising and its aftermath. Clanvisions, a company that makes extensive use of re-enactment or 'living history', produced a series of five programmes for Ulster Television.

The television productions in the south were *Rebellion* (RTÉ 1, producer Kevin Dawson, presenter Cathal O'Shannon) and *1798 agus Ó Shin/1798 and Since* (TnaG, producer Louis Marcus). *Rebellion* had Tom Bartlett, Kevin Whelan and Daire Keogh as historical consultants, and they produced a companion book – *Rebellion: a Television History* (Dublin, 1998). *Rebellion* appeared as three one-hour episodes on successive Wednesdays, 13, 20, 27 May

1998. Both southern productions featured contributions from the 'usual suspects', i.e. the historians of '98. The programmes also looked at the links with America and France, and in the case of *Rebellion*, time was spent time filming in those countries.

1798 WEBSITES

Numerous websites were set up for the bicentenary, many of which have closed down since. These include:

- Ballymoney Borough Council's 1798 website – www.1798ballymoney.org.uk
- Antrim Borough Council's website (www.antrim.gov.uk) has pages on the Battle of Antrim
- the Irish Government maintains its commemoration website on www.irlgov.ie/taoiseach/1798
- The National Archives, Bishop Street, Dublin has a 1798 site at www.national archives.ie
- a Republican-oriented site may be found at http://home-pages.iol.ie/~fagann/1798/index.html
- the Linen Hall Library website on 1798 is temporarily out of commission at the time of writing; for an update contact the Linen Hall Library, Belfast, on (028) 90321707 or try visiting www.linenhall.com.

An interactive CD-ROM, *Myth and Memory 1798*, was produced with CRC support by the Nerve Centre, 7–8 Magazine Street, Derry, BT48 6HJ. This complements *Who Fears to Speak?*, produced with Government support by Martello in 1998 in Dublin.

MURALS

While Belfast and other areas in the north are renowned for their political and cultural gable-wall murals, there has been an unaccountable paucity of those relating to '98. Exceptions have been murals on the Catholic New Lodge Road depicting United Irish Presbyterians, Dr Drennan, Rev. Steel Dickson, and Henry Joy McCracken and his sister, Mary Ann. A fine scenic mural in South Link, in Nationalist Andersonstown, shows pikemen marching through what appears to be a western landscape of mountains and lakes. In the grounds of the Roddy McCorley Club in the Nationalist Glen Road, Belfast, is a reproduction of John Carey's famous Battle of Antrim painting. A rare postmodern example, in Ardoyne, commemorates the mural painted there for the sesquicentenary of Robert Emmet in 1953. An illustration of the cross-community nature of the bicentenary commemorations is the series of murals in the town of Ballynahinch, scene of one of the bloodiest battles of 1798 (see Down District section above).

6

Epilogue

Cover of Dublin 1798 Commemoration Committee,
1948 pamphlet

Recent Writing on '98

A number of seminal publications were responsible for a revival of interest in the United Irishmen. In the 1950s, Charles Dickson was almost a lone voice with his studies of the Rising in Wexford and in the north. At the beginning of the 1960s, Mary McNeill produced an influential biography of Mary Ann McCracken, sister of Henry Joy.[113] This has gone into several reprints, most recently in the lead-up to the bicentenary. At the other end of the decade, Thomas Pakenham produced what was, for a long time, the most authoritative account of '98, though in many respects it has been superseded and even debunked.[114] This is in the nature of things, and indeed Pakenham himself brought out a revised and illustrated version in 1997, obviously in anticipation of bicentenary interest.

The play *Northern Star* by the late Stewart Parker, a northern Protestant, created a great deal of interest on its first Belfast appearance in 1984. Taking its title from the Belfast United Irish paper, *Northern Star* was an exploration of the radical and separatist politics of Ulster in the 1790s, through its main character Henry Joy McCracken. In its exposure of historic sectarianism, and by holding up the aims and ideals of the United Irishmen, it posited a message for its own day. It was revived triumphantly by the Tinderbox and Field Day Theatre Companies, in a Stephen Rea production, in the eminently appropriate setting of Rosemary Street Presbyterian Church as part of the 1998 Belfast Festival at Queen's.

The more recent crop of '98 books was ushered in by works in the 1980s by Wexford-born Trinity historian Louis Cullen, who looked at his own county with the eyes of a social historian. Thus the social composition and motivations of the forces involved in '98 were put under the searchlight of modern scholarship.[115] Ground-breaking works by Belfast-born Marianne Elliott introduced the 1790s to a wider audience.[116] A.T.Q. Stewart, the Queen's University historian, produced a number of influential books on '98 in Antrim and Down.[117] Tom Bartlett has also introduced new vistas into the study of the 1790s.[118] Nancy Curtin's study was sceptical of the idea that Protestant and Catholic rebels in '98 were universally working towards the same ideals and ends.[119] Kevin Whelan has broken new ground in the study of the United Irishmen and in reclaiming their memory.[120] Daire Keogh co-edited with Nicholas Furlong a recent excellent collection on the previously neglected role of women in '98.[121]

Many excellent works on localities were produced in anticipation of the bicentenary. These included Brendan McEvoy, *The United Irishmen in Tyrone* (Armagh, 1998); Kenneth Robinson, *North Down and Ards in 1798* (Bangor, 1998); W. Wilsdon, *The Sites of the 1798 Rising in Antrim and Down* (Belfast 1997); Peadar Bates, *1798 Rebellion in Fingal* (Fingal, 1998); Liam Chambers, *Rebellion in Kildare 1798–1803* (Dublin, 1998); Gerard MacAtasney, *Leitrim and the Croppies 1776–1804* (Carrick-on-Shannon, 1998); Peter O'Shaughnessey (ed.), *Rebellion in Wicklow: General Joseph Holt's Personal Account of 1798* (Dublin, 1998); and Ruan O'Donnell, *The Rebellion in Wicklow 1798* (Dublin, 1998). Two very well received collections, containing much new writing by local and academic historians, were produced to cover the phases of the Rising in Wexford and Down.[122] Allan Blackstock ploughed a comparatively lonely furrow with his comprehensive study of the Irish Yeomanry, the battlefield opponents of the United Irishmen.[123] 'History Ireland', edited by the scholar and enthusiast of the United Irishmen Tommy Graham, naturally produced an excellent commemorative edition containing important articles on '98, and information about the bicentenary.[124]

Commemoration itself became something of a historiographical battleground between two of Ireland's foremost historians, Professors Roy Foster and Tom Bartlett. This was occasioned by a chapter titled 'Remembering 1798' in the former's book.[125] A response by Bartlett challenged Foster on his attitude to the involvement of historians in commemoration of the Famine and, particularly, 1798.[126]

At one level Foster is attacking a recent phenomenon that has given rise to unease among historians, namely the 'Disneyfication' of history. This is manifest in a plethora of sometimes ill-thought-out interpretative centres and events involving 're-enactors'. In some cases, the process has lacked academic rigour and the motivation has been tourism and/or local particularism. The less well-founded of these have proved ephemeral and have gone to the wall. Others, however, have put down strong roots and, along with Ireland's earlier tradition of summer schools, have buoyed interest in history, both local and national. Foster is dubious of the validity of this phenomenon, especially where he sees it occurring in relation to the '98 bicentenary. He is somewhat disparaging of 'spectator sport' and 'commercialised theme-park' history. This encompasses 'the Puppet Show of '98' in Fingal; the Wexford Senate; the National Centre for Convict Transportation in the old Wicklow Gaol; the re-enactments of the battles of Ballinamuck and Carrignagart, complete with muskets; and, most of all, the return of the French in 1998 in the form of 'lycra-clad bicyclists' participating in the Tour de France, the first leg of which was in Ireland that year.[127]

More contentiously, Foster was concerned at the:

> extent to which professional historians were involved in the repackaging alterations of emphasis. There seemed, in some quarters at least, to be an agreed agenda which owed more to perceived late-twentieth-century needs than to a close reading of events and attitudes two hundred years ago.[128]

He quotes a speech delivered by Fine Gael minister Avril Doyle on 24 November 1995 announcing future plans for the commemoration:

> Firstly we much discard the now discredited sectarian version of '98, which was merely a polemical post-rebellion falsification. Secondly, we must stress the modernity of the United Irish project, its forward-looking, democratic dimension, and abandon the outdated or agrarian or peasant interpretation. Thirdly, we must emphasise the essential unity of the 1798 insurrection: what happened in Wexford was of a piece with what happened in Antrim and Down.[129]

He then quotes an almost verbatim extract from Fianna Fáil minister Síle de Valera's speech on 25 May 1998 (at the opening of the

National Museum's 1798 Exhibition at Collins Barracks), and cites cross-party 'reading from the same script'.[130]

Foster is not impressed by what he sees as attempts by politicians and/or historians to elide accounts of sectarianism from 1798, particularly in Wexford. He devotes considerable space to berating what he calls 'commemorationist' historians for their 'selective' memory in utilising contemporary sources in the reinterpretation of the events of 1798. At the same time, Foster himself goes to considerable pains to refute the official view, enlisting in turn both contemporary sources and present-day historians that coincide with his own views.

Inevitably, Foster's bicentenary-debunking exercise drew a rejoinder from among those targeted. One of Foster's assertions was that 'the historians retained by the government for the purpose of commemoration, and sent forth on a mission, acted up to the mark'.[131] Tom Bartlett, speaking 'as one of those historians "retained" by the Irish government', retorted, 'To this sad charge, I can only echo Standish O'Grady's "were you momentarily mad, or living in London when you wrote this?".'[132] Bartlett vigorously rejects Foster's assertion 'that sectarianism was deliberately ignored' by historians commemorating the bicentenary. He castigates him for his somewhat snide assaults on some of the more popular aspects of the bicentenary, accusing him in turn of elitism:

> It is the duty of the historian of Ireland … to explain to audiences of all types, not just academic but 'popular' … as well, what he or she is about, and to enter into discussion with them. It is simply not good enough for Professor Foster to assail those Irish historians who attempt to reach out beyond the ivory tower in order to inform and educate the ordinary public. For Irish historians not to do so would mean inevitably conceding 'Irish history' and 'commemoration' to the crank and monomaniac and to those who are agenda-driven and politically engaged.[133]

In both these contributions there is more than an echo of the divisions and confrontational style that has bedevilled Irish historiography for years. For our purposes Foster's piece acts as a reminder that not everyone, including leading historians, was at one in commemorating the bicentenary of '98.

What they said about the bicentenary

The bicentenary's leading lights, unlike those of previous anniversaries, were mainly not politically motivated. This time the main events were organised by historians (national and local), council officials and community workers. Leading participants were asked by me to reflect on the bicentenary as they saw it. Their comments were as follows (in alphabetical order).

Damien Brannigan
(Community Relations Officer, Down District Council and leading organiser of '98 Programme in Down):

The bicentenary in our area was very successful. We had a good cross-community committee, made up of representatives from the voluntary, community, statutory and education sectors, which acted as a co-ordinating body. This committee had the unanimous support and backing of all the political parties in Down District Council.

Forty local bodies spread throughout the District, and from different religious, political and cultural backgrounds, organised over 50 projects …

The events were positively received and very well attended by the public. None of the events generated any negative reaction. The press and public were very supportive of the approach the Council adopted towards marking the occasion and this is reflected in the press cuttings …

Articles by local and professional historians examining the events leading to, during and following the 1798 Rebellion were featured in our three local papers, the *Mourne Observer*, *Down Recorder*, and *Down Democrat*. Unfortunately, we did not keep cuttings of these.

Gauging by the attendance, enthusiasm and contribution at events it could be said that the bicentenary commemorations in Down District inspired or revived people's appetite for information on the 1798 Rising.

Bernard Browne
(Comóradh '98, Director National 1798 Centre Enniscorthy):

The challenge facing Comóradh '98 in the early days of the organisation (it had been set up by Enniscorthy Urban Council and

Wexford County Council in late 1987) was not to let it become 'the bulletin board' for any sector. The mission statement stated that it was to be: a suitable, dignified and appropriate commemoration. The story of 1798 has been blessed with a wealth of fine reference works, perhaps in part because of the complexity of the story. The combination of historical romance and the macabre also attracted widespread interest in the fiction of 1798.

The rapid changes in the historiography of the United Irishmen and the story of the rebellion and the pole-vaulting over many of 'traditional' narratives and the postmillennial ideology of the secular gospel of progress disturbed many of the local organisers. To judge by the newspaper headlines and letters to the press, the secular approach and historical advances to the commemoration ideals worked. A broad consensus developed between historians and academics as well as Government on how the commemoration should take place. The rival visions had political resonance; there was no shortage of ideology from some political machines.

The background to the Belfast talks in early 1998 also helped. No longer were people prisoners to a created culture of 1798. Historians and librarians unearthed, collected, exhibited and analysed the real story of 1798. A level of scholarship arose that had not been seen before. Lecture halls and conferences became sources of spontaneity and passion as gifted amateurs and experts set about recovering the real story of 1798. The traditional biography of 1798 got short shrift. Over 100 books were published to mark the bicentennial; many writers relied heavily on memoirs, unofficial sources and other written material. Some 850 events took place from Beverley Hills to Carrig on Bannow, from Sydney to Paris.

There was also a cultural tourism and economic pull to the commemoration. Many historians' criticism of the cultural tourist side of 1798 often verged on the shrill. The marketing mix of 1798 had to include something for everyone. Comóradh '98 controlled its marketing, trademarking of logos and merchandising to a large extent. The creed of capitalist realism was needed to part finance the overall commemoration and create a public awareness. This is a consumer culture.

Deep emotions were at play; no one had any illusions, that a lengthy period of adjustment and adaptation were needed before anyone would feel comfortable with the commemoration. The transition began slowly, there was a growing demand for lectures, the role of women in 1798 was investigated, ambitious local historians published widely on their areas' involvement in the campaign.

An important point to be noted was that in counties that were the main theatres of the 1798 summer campaign, the Local Authorities followed the lead of Wexford County Council in organising key events. This was done as funding was needed and 1798 was also looked upon as a prime cultural tourism and economic asset. The economic and tourism side stirred considerable comment among scholars.

For the most part, the commemorations were suitable and dignified; there were no quixotic commemorations of lost Croppy Graves. The iconoclasts looked to the Pike as the most potent symbol of 1798. Although its design caused more controversy, as different counties produced their own versions.

The many myths that came to enshroud 1798 and the United Irishmen were removed. Many different organisations and groups were active in the commemoration; the quest for truth in history is an old one. Grappling with a complex story proved to be a challenge, the old blessed trinity of 1898 celebrations: Boolavogue, Fr Murphy and Vinegar Hill were discarded and placed in a modern context.

The years 1997–8 were the perfect climate for the expansion of our understanding of 1798, the ongoing negotiations of the Belfast or Good Friday Agreement, the completion of the Comóradh '98 programme also helped.

The public fixation on such episodes as the Scullabogue Barn, Carnew and Wexford Bridge massacres frustrated some historians as the message of the United Irishmen was lost on some.

For the most part, the veil was lifted, the intellectual revolution that began with Charles Dickson in the 1950s and which continued with Professor Louis Cullen brought forth new history. A series of radical changes coupled with our cultural evolution created a stir, but not a revolution, the old polemical style remained in some quarters.

A framework in a series of lectures and published papers provided advances in the new thinking on 1798. The biggest single problem was the magnitude of the number of casualties in 1798. Academics such as Dr Marianne Elliott gave figures of upwards of

50,000 people; other historians such as Dr Kevin Whelan give figures of 30,000. Other leading figures question these figures as
excessive. The data for the higher figures appears to be extreme.
This is a healthy turn of events, as it means the real revolution of
1798 is only now beginning as historians continue to modify their
research.

The United Irishmen and 1798 will always have a diversity of
scholarly enterprise and point of view. The long historical struggle
with the historiography of the most complex decade in our modern history will ensure that the ideals of the United Irish: *Liberté,
Egalité et Fraternité* will continue to prosper.

David Hall

(historian, prominent organiser of events in Antrim,
author of a book on the Battle of Antrim, and schoolteacher):

This chance to cast a retrospective glance at how the rebellion of
1798 – 'The Turnout' – was commemorated, has proved to be very
enjoyable, as were so many of the events and projects which I was
fortunate to have attended or been involved with.

I have lived in Antrim for most of my life, teaching history in
Parkhall College, a local secondary school, for the last eight years.
My interest in the rebellion and the battle in particular began at the
start of my teaching career. Our local subject for coursework at
GCSE was 'The Battle of Antrim', with the pupils answering questions on the context, the engagement and some of the characters
involved using a wide range of primary and secondary evidence.
(Unbelievably this local aspect was dropped from the syllabus in
1997 – the year before the bicentenary!) Teaching the topic led me
to ask many more questions about the battle which became
increasingly frustrating as the battle was only ever treated generally in the historiography of 1798. Even locally no-one had ever
written a single volume devoted solely to what is arguably the single most important event in the town's history. This was too good
an opportunity to miss.

What started off as a small scale project to write a 30-page pamphlet to explain to the locals the battle in its context snowballed as
my fascination increased. My research subsequently brought me
into contact with many who also wished to commemorate the
events of '98. A meeting called by Antrim Borough Council on the
27th of May 1997 saw the formation of a steering committee to

oversee the various commemorative events. Even at this early stage it was clear to everyone the potential of what lay ahead, inspired and encouraged by John Gray of the Linen Hall Library who addressed those who attended that evening.

On the 14th of October 1997 I was privileged to be invited to two events at the Old Presbyterian Church at Templepatrick to commemorate the 200th anniversary of the execution of William Orr, who lived on the outskirts of Antrim in the townland of Farrashane. 'Remember Orr' became the battle-cry of many rebels in Ulster in '98. In the afternoon, the Remember Orr Co-ordinating Committee unveiled a new grave marker at Orr's grave in the old graveyard of the church, now part of the Upton estate. In the evening this most beautiful of old churches was packed to hear music, poetry and prose from the era, as well as reflections on the man himself. In 1798 the church was used to hide an old Volunteer cannon which was unearthed in the days prior to the outbreak in Ulster, fired, though ineffectively, in the Battle of Antrim.

The Battle of Antrim was also commemorated by using the very latest technology with the opening of an Interactive Website in January 1998. This was the brainchild of local teacher and historian Alastair Smyth and allows the user to investigate many aspects of the battle and its participants, and is still available by visiting the website of Antrim Borough Council.

My own sense of achievement was realised on the 27th of March 1998 with the launch of my book *A Battle Lost and Won*. The title comes from a poem I found in the Bigger Collection in Belfast Central Library by T.C.S. Corry, written in the nineteenth century called 'Reminiscence of '98':

My father held a little farm, not far from broad Lough Neagh,
    And Mem'ry oft recalls again, that bright but fatal day,
When pike and sword in deadly feud, flashed in the noontide sun,
    And Antrim's peaceful town beheld a battle lost and won ...

Researching, writing and publishing the book brought many, many rewards. I was able to correspond with Mr Alan Carey of New York, the son of J.W. Carey who drew the famous line drawing of the battle of Antrim, used in many books since, back in the 1890s. I do not claim to be an expert but I have had the opportunity to lecture on the battle and its significance throughout Northern Ireland, coming into contact with the many people who strive to keep local history alive for future generations. I feel I have benefited from the research in reading the works of Pakenham, Dickson, Madden and others who have brought the era of rebellion to life, making me much more appreciative of the history of my country, my town and its people. I will always maintain that no understanding of the rebellion is complete without looking at Antrim and its participants, most notably James Hope the self-taught weaver–revolutionary who, to my mind, encapsulates more of the spirit of '98 than any other individual.

Undoubtedly, the crowning glory of the year was the re-enactment of the battle on Saturday 6th June 1998. First mentioned at that preliminary meeting just over twelve months before, the day itself proved to be more successful than anyone imagined. The idea was suggested by local man John Smyth, chairman of the Ulster Heritage Museum Committee who consistently believed the re-enactment could be realised, despite the doubts of many. We are very fortunate that many of the streets and buildings in Antrim remain from the period of rebellion, making the re-enactment even more realistic.

Thousands packed the streets of the town from around noon and a break in the rain seemed almost heaven-sent as the planned and choreographed timetable of events swung into action. Many of those who gave up their time and who participated in the re-run of 'the turnout' were Orangemen – serving not only as yeomen and members of His Majesty's dragoons but also as rebels. Local shops, cafes and pubs, of all persuasions and none, joined in, with many dressing in period costume, as did I. I feel privileged to have been involved as the commentator on the day, sampling so much of the wonderful atmosphere in the town, perched on the back of a trailer with the Mayor of the Borough, Paddy Marks – we had the best view in town.

The next day saw a more placid remembrance of the battle on its 200th anniversary with a service of commemoration in All Saints Parish Church. which was itself a focal point in the engagement two centuries before. Afterwards, the congregation walked down High Street through Market Square to the Castle Wall, defended by local yeomen against local United Irishmen in '98, where the Mayor unveiled a commemorative plaque inscribed to the memory of all who fought that day.

The last of the events in which I was personally involved saw four local schools come together to visually capture various aspects of battle two hundred years ago. I addressed pupils from the four schools – Parkhall College, Massareene Community College, St Malachy's High and St Olcan's High – before the young artists set about creating wonderfully colourful and imaginative tapestries showing prominent scenes from the battle which were then mounted on the windows of the old Market House in Antrim in time for the bicentenary. The project, like so many funded by the local council, was rewarded with the presentation of an 'Interpret Ireland History Award' in 1999. This is a real credit to the many local children who worked so hard in what was a unique and fitting educational project.

Looking back, I feel that 1998 was both a memorable and enjoyable year for me (with my wife glad to see the start of 1999!), but most particularly for the people of Antrim, both young and old.

Rev. Brian Kennaway

(Presbyterian minister, Crumlin; former convenor of the Education Committee of the Grand Orange Lodge of Ireland):

For anyone to attempt to 'break new ground' in an institutional organisation is difficult enough. In an institution like the Orange Order, given its commitment to 'meddle not with them that are given to change' (Proverbs 24:21), it is well nigh impossible.

Attempting to be progressive and visionary, the Education Committee of the Grand Orange Lodge of Ireland in the early 1990s indicated to the Grand Lodge that something imaginative ought to be done to commemorate the bicentenary of the United Irishman's Rebellion of 1798.

The Committee proceeded, with the approval of the Grand Lodge, to publish two booklets. The first was *Murder Without Sin*, being edited extracts from the publication *Orangeism; Its Origin and History* by Ogle Robert Gowan, first published in Toronto 1859. This publication, which covered the Rebellion in Wexford, demonstrated how the rising quickly turned from the ideals of the United Irishmen to the ugly sectarian conflict, which defaced and eventually destroyed their cause. The title of this publication caused annoyance among some in the Republic. This was the representation of the letters 'M.W.S.' on the rebel flag carried at the massacre of Protestants on Wexford Bridge. We adhered to the

historical interpretation of the letters as 'Murder Without Sin' –
indicating that it was no sin to murder a Protestant because they
were heretics anyway.

The Committee also published another reprint, from the only
major official history of the Order – *The Sunshine Patriots: the
1798 Rebellion in Antrim & Down*. This was an excerpt from R.M.
Sibbett's *Orangeism in Ireland and throughout the Empire* (Thynne
& Co., 1938). County Antrim and County Down Grand Lodges
both supported the Education Committee in this project and took
responsibility for the sale of 3,000 and 5,000 copies respectively. It
was the large print-run of this publication which facilitated the
Committee to finance the Commemorative Dinner on 12th June
1998. This enabled the Committee to invite and accommodate
guests from the Republic of Ireland and England. *The Sunshine
Patriots* was placed on the list of official publications recommended by the Department of Education for Northern Ireland; this we
believe was a first for the Order.

At the beginning of 1997, I expressed concern, to some Dublin
politicians, that the commemorations planned for the Republic of
Ireland should be inclusive and fully recognise the contribution of
the Orangemen of 1798.

This resulted in an invitation from the Minister of State at the
Department of the Taoiseach, Avril Doyle TD, to Leinster House,
Dublin on Wednesday 5th March 1997. It had become known
that the Orange Order, through its Education Committee, was
proposing to commemorate the 1798 Rebellion and reflect upon
its significance for Irish Protestants. Naturally this was of great
interest to the Southern constituency. With the Minister, to discuss
the commemoration of the 1798 Rebellion, over lunch, were
Professor Tom Bartlett, the Irish Government's Adviser on 1798,
and Senator Dr Mary Henry.

The Committee had decided on 28th February that David
Richardson and myself should be present to represent the
Committee. This visit caused some media interest and heightened
the profile of the Institution. Although it was made clear to
reporters outside Leinster House that our interest was purely academic and historical, the manner in which this was reported by the
BBC added to the misunderstanding. Clearly a greater maturity
was required on both sides of the border, but it was the 'flat-earth-
ers' among the Orange constituency who gave most cause for

concern. They confused the geographical transition to Dublin with a political conversion to republican politics.

Our interest in the Commemoration of the 1798 Rebellion led to invitations to write articles for various publications, including the *Irish Times* and the *Irish Catholic*. We took part in a Gaelic television programme on the Rebellion and were commended by the perceptive Irish journalist Eoghan Harris in his *Sunday Times* article of 6th September 1998 – 'Some contributors were convincing – Brian Kennaway, Louis Cullen and Breandan O Buachalla ...'. All this helped to improve the public perception of the Institution and present the more reasonable, if not academic, image.

Of course not everyone in the Orange Order was pleased with our efforts. Some who would have thought nothing of going to Landsdowne Road, Dublin, and standing for the 'Soldier's Song', severely criticised the Education Committee for making the Orange viewpoint known to members of the Dublin establishment. But then, hypocritical cant is often used in place of rational argument.

The major event in the Orange contribution to the commemorations of 1798 as far as the Education Committee was concerned, was the Commemorative Dinner, held on 12th June 1998 in Parliament Buildings, Stormont. The Grand Lodge had two years previously given permission to the Education Committee to organise a Dinner. The significance of Friday 12th June 1998 is that this was the Friday between the Battle of Antrim on 6th June, and the Battle of Ballynahinch on 13th June.

Only one person objected, Joel Patton. The leader of the 'Spirit of Drumcree' faction, in his usual aggressive fashion objected to the Mayor of Dublin attending the Dinner. The Mayor in fact wore the Chain of Office presented to the Corporation of the City of Dublin by William III, of 'glorious', pious and immortal memory'.

In spite of the lack of understanding and the stumbling blocks presented in our way the Commemoration Dinner went ahead with 91 people attending. There were 30 invited guests, 13 of them from the Irish Republic. Academia, taking in all the major Irish Universities, and journalism were well represented. Professor Brian Walker gave an excellent After Dinner Lecture on 'The Lessons of '98'. He concluded his Lecture in words reminiscent of R.M. Sibbett, by reminding his hearers that they should also recall the brave Catholic soldiers of the Monaghan militia who fought and died to save Ireland for the Crown and those gallant Presbyterian United Irishmen who fought and died for a new Ireland.

Sponsorship for the project had been received from Co-Operation North, The Community Relations Council: Cultural Diversity Programme, The Northern Ireland Tourist Board and Edenderry Print. If the success of the evening is to be measured by the number of positive and encouraging letters which followed, then, it was a resounding success.

The great fault of all this was that the Education Committee were being both positive and progressive. That to some was a 'double fault'. But there is a price to be paid for vision and courage, and that will no doubt be revealed in the coming months.[134]

Daire Keogh

(academic historian, writer and much-requested speaker on 1798):

Few could have anticipated how the 1798 bicentenary commemorations would have gone. On one level, all of us with an interest in history were familiar with the great 'celebrations' in the past. There were powerful images of the events of 1898, impressive gatherings in Wexford, the colour of the Fenians with pikes, the wonderful sculpture of Oliver Sheppard, permanent memorials to the great campaign for Faith and Fatherland. The film footage of 1948, too, High Masses on battle sites, the climb to the Cave Hill, all of the events reflected an enthusiasm and certainty and a situation of 1798 within a very specific political context and tradition.

It was never certain how the events of 1998 would go. Yes there was a tendency to bring the enthusiasm of the peace process to the commemorations. In particular, events and publications tended to stress the inclusive nature of the United Irish project; above all Tone's brave hope to unite the creeds under the common name of Irishman took on a particular significance as if the United Irishmen were party to the Good Friday Agreement. Certainly such tendencies were over-simplistic, but how could people not draw parallels given the great hopes in 1998 to leave our bloody past and divisions behind us?

In a similar way, the spirit of the time dictated that commemorations would be ecumenical in spirit – for many that cross-community element was most significant and brought home sharply the extent to which '98 had been hijacked by Catholic Nationalists in the past.

I'm not sure to what extent the commemorations impacted on the population as a whole. Certainly events were well attended – Vinegar Hill Sunday in Enniscorthy brought tens of thousands to the streets. Valiant efforts were made by local community groups to mount commemorative events, but outside of the theatres which saw action in 1798 there was little enthusiasm for such enterprises. Nevertheless, in the parish halls, libraries and schools locals were interested in debating 1798 – in broadening their geographical sense of the Rebellion and attempting to contextualise the year in its international setting. Personally, that was the most satisfactory element of the commemoration, the way in which the inspiration of the United Irishmen, neglected in the earlier celebrations, was placed at the heart of 1998. Of course, critics saw this intellectualisation of the inspiration of the Rebellion as an attempt to play down the embarrassing excesses of 1798, the sectarian element and the well-documented massacres. These aspects of '98 were not ignored and figured prominently in the invaluable publications produced to mark the occasion. Many fine local studies were completed which broadened the geographical sense of 1798 and new constituencies were addressed, particularly the seriously neglected women of '98.

The commemorations were an experience never to be forgotten – difficult to explain. I remember one beautiful August evening in Monaseed, following hundreds of 'pikemen' along a country road, the sun coming through the trees above. It was amazing – and the women, dressed in eighteenth-century attire, accompanied by children carrying rabbits on their shoulders. Yes, it was reminiscent of Heaney's 'Requiem for the Croppy'. You could question the historical accuracy of such commemorations, but no one with a soul could fail to be moved.

A.T.Q. Stewart

(former QUB academic historian, author of influential books and prominent speaker on 1798):

At a reception in Dublin in 1982 to mark the bicentenary of Grattan's Parliament I got into conversation with a well known Nationalist MP on the subject of commemoration. It was not our first meeting. We had a camaraderie that derived from being members of that travelling circus which in the 1970s aired the distresses of Northern Ireland before audiences in Oxford and London, New York and Washington. I asked him what he thought would happen in 1998. To my surprise he shuddered and said 'I just hope that I am not around then'. To some extent I shared his apprehension. In 1898 there had been serious riots in Ballynahinch and Belfast, in which a hundred policemen were injured, and the co-religionists of Betsy Gray had sledge-hammered her monument to pieces and attacked the charabancs of Home Rulers converging on it. Happily, we were both still around in 1998, each remembering 1798 in his own way, and able to witness that in general the commemoration of the Great Rebellion/Rising had been a success, and had passed off in an atmosphere of tolerance and good humour. Though there were undoubtedly disorders in the North, these were tightly focused on Drumcree, and apparently not related to the bicentenary.

A torrent of books poured from Irish presses and swamped the bookshops. There were two enormously impressive exhibitions, one organised by the National Library and the National Museum of Ireland at Collins Barracks in Dublin, and the other by the Ulster Museum in Belfast, with the support of Belfast City Council. Each was complemented by the production of a lavishly illustrated book of record, the harvest of the scholarly labours of Professor Kevin Whelan and Dr W.A. Maguire respectively. These volumes will be standard works of reference for many years to come. Centres like Enniscorthy and Wexford mounted elaborate events of commemoration, and smaller towns all over Ireland arranged exhibitions, lectures and conferences. The study of local history received a considerable stimulus. And let us not forget the omnipotent influence of television, which (such is the nature of the medium) sometimes undermined the historians by sowing new errors and confusions.

How are we to explain the good feeling? It would be tempting to think that people in the North had other distractions. The fragile ceasefire was holding. The 'peace process' was nearing its most critical and dangerous phase. A great deal of effort was being put into convincing people that 1798 was not relevant to their present situation; that, in Tony Blair's view, history was rubbish. In fact exactly the opposite influence may have been at work; the parallels were too close for comfort. In the North the Presbyterians reoccupied their history. The little church at Templepatrick was packed to overflowing on the evening when, to the accompaniment of Irish harps, the congregation remembered the 'martyrdom' of William Orr. After all, his remains lay in their churchyard, and the cannon fired at Antrim had once been concealed beneath the pews in which they sat. My own impression was that they did not identify too much with what was happening in Enniscorthy, and that to most people in the south television's revelation that the revolt in the North had been almost entirely a Presbyterian affair came as something of a culture shock. The fact that Presbyterians actually looked back on it with pride was confusing. Add to this that some Orangemen believed that what they were commemorating was the putting down of the Rebellion.

So everyone seemed to derive some satisfaction from the anniversary. When I wrote a book about the Rising in Antrim and Down (published in 1997 but contemplated for three decades) I received many letters from people whose ancestors had been out in 1798. None was hostile, and all were seeking more information, perhaps in the belief that I was actually there! There are, of course, some in both communities in the North who, for different reasons, viewed the extent of Presbyterian involvement with some embarrassment. Neither they, nor the bulk of the population in the Republic are disposed to agree with Mr Blair that history should be written off as a bad debt. One is left with the feeling that in 1998 we were all commemorating in our own inimitable and all-too-familiar way.

Kevin Whelan

(Smurfit Director Keough-University of Notre Dame Centre, Dublin) was one of the leading movers in the 1798 bicentenary. He was a much-requested speaker at events north and south and as far afield as Australia and the USA. He wrote of the year of commemoration as follows:

> I dwell in possibility.
>   *Emily Dickinson*

It was a great year. Nobody could have predicted beforehand that the Bicentenary would be celebrated so passionately, would stimulate such massive community involvement, or take place in a political atmosphere where the bitter miasma of three decades seemed to be suddenly lifting and clearing. Neither could it have been anticipated that the commemorations would be marked by a mature, positive and sophisticated understanding of the principles of the United Irishmen. In retrospect, the groundwork had been well laid by a decade of solid research and reinterpretation of the 1790s, spearheaded by Louis Cullen, Marianne Elliott and Tom Bartlett, and carried on by a gifted cohort of younger scholars. The 1790s replaced the seventeenth century as the hot area of Irish history. The high quality of publication broadened the discussion well beyond the narrow and rancorous revisionist debate and opened a hospitable intellectual space, marked by civility and co-operation. The stray discordant voices – isolated in Cork, Oxford, Wisconsin – were still stuck in the trenches of 1980s debate while the active generation of '98 scholars seriously and persistently engaged with each other, but also crucially with local communities.

By the time that 1998 came around, a bracing new air had swept through the moth-eaten older version of 1798. Its calcified certainties, sour sectarianism and reductionism were gradually but decisively redefined in favour of more nuanced, open-ended and infinitely richer interpretations. On the scholarly front, a gratifying array of new work appeared, some of it destined to stand the test of time. The three-volume Drennan–McTier correspondence, Volume I of the *Collected Tone* and an accessible edition of Tone's *Life* stand out from many impressive publications.

It was a privilege to be personally involved in 120 different Bicentenary events, all of them worthwhile, many of them deeply moving, some indelibly imprinted in imagination and memory. My own highlights include a sweltering May day in my native village of Clonegal; here, I felt the hand of history, at the evocative sight of glittering pikeheads swaying over the hedgerows as the serried parishes made their own of 1798. I thought of Keats's Adonis: 'The dead live there/and move like winds of light on dark and stormy air.' I thought too of my own direct ancestors on either side of the '98 divide – Thomas Bookey (immortalised and misrepresented in P.J. McCall's stirring anthem 'Boolavogue') and the croppy blacksmith Carton of Scarawalsh Crossroads.

The quality of public monuments also improved dramatically in the Bicentenary. Two highlights would be the dignified environmentally themed monument at the hitherto scandalously neglected Croppies' Acre on the Liffey, and the visionary Tulach an tSolais on Oulart Hill – Michael Warren's modern megalith, cleft down the middle to allow access to a cool, clear, pure interior chamber, and aligned so that the rising solstice sun shines directly through it onto Vinegar Hill, scene of the decisive battle on that hot summer's day on 21 June 1798. Cultural highlights were Stephen Rea's brilliant production of Stewart Parker's *Northern Star* in the resonant setting of Rosemary Street Presbyterian church in Belfast, Medbh McGuckian's characteristic blend of ellipsis, emotion and imagination in her 1798-themed collection *Shelmalier* and the reprinting of the *Poor Man's Cathecism* – an underground classic of Irish radicalism

On a more private tack, a black note was Johnny Dooley's last-gasp goal which scuppered Wexford's '98 campaign – all the more galling in that I had been asked to give a pep-talk to the team beforehand. This was by far the toughest thing I did in 1998 – and at least I had the satisfaction of being told later by Adrian Fenlon that the hairs were standing on the back of his neck after my presentation. A more pleasant memory was Seamus Heaney's graceful launch of my *Fellowship of Freedom* book in the Ferrycarrig Hotel – a Derryman steeped in '98 gloriously at home among the Yellabellies.

Finally there was an almost tangible sense in 1998 that two centuries of frozen politics were melting and that the United Irishmen's time had come around once more, that their song was returning with the season. As James Hope, the veteran and uncowed Presbyterian United Irishman from Templepatrick, wrote towards the end of his exemplary life:

> 'Physical force may prevail for a time but there is music in the sound of moral force which will be heard like the sound of the cuckoo. The bird lays its eggs, and leaves them for a time; but it will come again and hatch them in due course, and the song will return with the season'.

After the event

At the start of this book I stated that the initiative for the work had come from the award to me of a Cultural Traditions Fellowship by the Community Relations Council (CRC). The work prescribed in the Fellowship was twofold. I was asked to write a book on commemoration of '98 historically, and in particular to record the bicentenary events. Also, I was to get involved in the bicentenary events as an organiser of the United Irishmen Commemoration Society (UICS). CRC asked that I record what it was hoped would be the cross-community nature of the bicentenary, as opposed to the divisiveness such commemorations had fomented in the past. Secondly, I was actively to promote cross-community involvement in the commemoration of '98, particularly among Protestant and Unionist communities which had been lukewarm or actively opposed to it in the past. This I did largely through my work with UICS.

Nevertheless, such communities needed no such encouragement as they enthusiastically reclaimed and celebrated their heritage, which for historic reasons had been obscured or suppressed. This was especially marked in the large programmes initiated by Unionist-controlled councils. That interest, indeed devotion, was manifest in the north in the vast number of events staged right across the community. I would point to my calendar of events for the bicentenary as undeniable proof that this is the case. As such, there is a sharp contrast with the centenary year, when the events of '98 in the north were commemorated in nationalist areas that had hardly been touched in 1798, whereas in unionist areas of Antrim and Down they were met with indifference or hostility.

Where northern Nationalists commemorated the bicentenary of '98 there was a marked lack of partisanship and a reaching out to the community as a whole. This was also the case in the south, not least in the pronouncements emanating from government ministers reaching out to northern Protestants. Also, it might be said that the mood music that attended the ushering in of the Good Friday Agreement in 1998 was the same for cross-community commemoration of '98.

That the CRC's cross-community aspirations came to fruition is due in no small part to the very active and enthusiastic UICS, which is in its own membership truly a microcosm reflecting the intense interest in '98 throughout all communities. Commemorative events continue after 1998. On 1 October 1999 a plaque to Henry Joy McCracken was unveiled at Joy's Entry, High Street, Belfast, adjacent to his place of execution in 1798. The blue ceramic plaque was commissioned by the Ulster History Circle, a body that erects such plaques at appropriate sites in memory of prominent Ulster people. The plaque bears the Circle's name with the legend 'Henry Joy McCracken 1767–1798, United Irishman born in a house near this site'. The event received £500 in support from Belfast City Council and the Community Relations Council. The plaque was unveiled by Belfast Lord Mayor, Councillor Bob Stoker, who stated that 'It gives me great pleasure on behalf of the people of the city and as a Unionist to unveil this.' Interestingly, the *Irish News* commented that 'Unionists previously confused as to their official stance towards Henry Joy McCracken, have backed plans by the Ulster History Circle to honour the patriot – 201 years after he was hanged ... despite a council decision four years ago, refusing permission to another historical society (Glenravel Local History Project) seeking to erect a similar memorial.'

The United Irishmen Commemoration Society, Belfast, is continuing to address issues related to '98 such as the bicentenary of the Act of Union. The society organised a very successful weekend visit to Wexford from Friday 1 October to Sunday 3 October 1999. Based at Murphy Flood's Hotel, Enniscorthy, the party of 35 visited the National 1798 Centre in that town, as well as the battlefields of Co. Wexford. Acquaintanceships were renewed with fellow '98 enthusiasts in the county, some of whom have been regular visitors to the commemorative events in the north. So successful was this that further trips were organised to the scenes of the Humbert campaign in the west in October 2000 and Wicklow/Kildare in October 2002. In October 1999, the society held its annual conference in Central Hall, Rosemary Street Presbyterian Church. The theme was 'Strategies for Survival', on the aftermath of the 1798 rising. Speakers included John Gray, Finlay Holmes, Daire Keogh, Ruan O'Donnell, Philip Orr and Kevin Whelan, and an evening of music of the '98 period and its commemoration followed. On 24 June 2002 at Rosemary Street Presbyterian Church, Belfast, under the auspices of the Ulster History Circle, a blue ceramic plaque was unveiled by Mayor Alex Maskey to Dr William Drennan, the ideologue of the United Irishmen. Drennan was a son of the manse of that particular church. Drennan's own son was a strong Unionist, which typified the drift within the families of many Presbyterian United Irishmen after '98.

UICS committee member Dr Raymond Shearer brought to fruition his scheme for a large bronze plaque to Henry Joy McCracken. Raymond was entirely and solely responsible for collecting donations and commissioning this. The large plaque shows the year 1798 around a profile of Henry Joy with crossed pikes below. Underneath, the inscription reads:

Henry Joy McCracken
Radical Belfast Presbyterian
Hanged At Cornmarket For
Leading the United Irishmen At The
Battle of Antrim 7 June 1798

"Faithful To The Last"

The plaque is now positioned at the entrance to the Provincial Masonic Hall, 15 Rosemary Street, Belfast. As Henry Joy McCracken, like many United Irishmen, was a Freemason, a member of Lodge 783, this is entirely appropriate. The plaque was unveiled at a ceremony on Tuesday, 4 February 2003 jointly by Sinn Fein Mayor of Belfast Alex Maskey and Provincial Grand Master R.W. Bro. A.J. McKinley. This ceremony and the broad backgrounds of those coming together in it speaks volumes on how commemoration of the United Irishmen is now the joint property of all communities in the north, if indeed from different perspectives. Thus, the

Bronze head by John Neill
PRODUCED BY *CAST*, DUBLIN

United Irishmen and their philosophy continue to have an impact which is more than purely historical and which speaks down the generations.

Bronze pikemen, Fuascailt monument on N25,
Co. Wexford, 1998

Bibliography

BOOKS

Bartlett, Thomas, *The Fall and Rise of the Irish Nation: the Catholic Question 1690–1830* (Dublin, 1992).

Bartlett, Thomas (ed.), *Life of Theobald Wolfe Tone*, compiled and arranged by William Theobald Wolfe Tone (Dublin, 1998).

— Bartlett, T., Dickson, D., Keogh, D. and Whelan, K. (eds), *The 1798 Rebellion, a bicentenary perspective* (Dublin, 2003). This contains a huge bibliography on the United Irishmen and related topics.

Bates, Peadar, *1798 Rebellion in Fingal* (Fingal, 1998).

Bigger, Francis Joseph, *Remember Orr*, published as a historical facsimile by the United Irish Commemoration Society (Belfast, 1998).

Blackstock, Allan, *An Ascendancy Army: the Yeomanry 1796–1834* (Dublin, 1998).

Byrne, Myles, *Memoirs* with a new introduction by Thomas Bartlett (Enniscorthy, 1998).

Cleary, Brian, *The Battle of Oulart Hill, 1798: Context and Strategy* (Naas, 1999).

Curtin, N.J. *The United Irishmen: Popular Politics in Ulster and Dublin* (Oxford, 1994).

Dickson, Charles, *Revolt in the North: Antrim and Down in 1798* (Dublin, 1960).

Dickson, Charles, *The Wexford Rising in 1798, Its Causes and Course* (Tralee, 1958).

Dickson, David, Keogh, Daire and Whelan, Kevin (eds), *The United Irishmen: Radicalism, Republicanism and Rebellion* (Dublin, 1993).

Elliott, Marianne, *Partners in Revolution: the United Irishmen and France* (New Haven, 1982).

Elliott, Marianne, *Wolfe Tone: Prophet of Irish Independence* (New Haven, 1989).

Foster, R.F., *The Irish Story: Telling Tales and Making It Up In Ireland* (London, 2001).

Gonne, Maud, *A Servant of the Queen* (Dublin, 1938).

Gray, John, *The Sans Culottes of Belfast* (Belfast, 1998).

Hall, David, *A Battle Lost and Won* (Antrim, 1798)

Hanna, Ronnie (ed.), *The Union: Essays on Ireland and the British Connection* (Newtownards, 2001).

Hill, Myrtle, Turner, Brian and Dawson, Kenneth, (eds), *The 1798
Rebellion in Down* (Newtownards, 1998).

Holmes, Finlay, *The Presbyterian Church in Ireland: a Popular History*
(Dublin, 2000).

Hope, James, *Autobiography of a Working Man*, reprinted with a new
introduction by Ian Adamson (Belfast, 1998).

Johnston, Sheila T., *Alice: a Life of Alice Milligan* (Omagh, 1994).

Kennedy, Brian P. and Gillespie, Raymond (eds) *Ireland: Art into History*
(Dublin, 1994).

Keogh, Daire and Furlong, Nicholas (eds), *The Mighty Wave: the 1798
Rebellion in Wexford* (Dublin, 1998).

Keogh, Daire and Furlong, Nicholas (eds), *The Women of 1798* (Dublin,
1998).

Killen, John, *The Decade of the United Irishmen, Contemporary Accounts
1791–1801* (Belfast, 1997).

Lawlor, Chris, *The Massacre on Dunlavin Green* (Naas, 1998).

Lyons, F.S.L., *Ireland Since the Famine* (London, 1973).

MacAtasney, Gerard, *Leitrim and the Croppies* (Carrick-on-Shannon,
1998).

McCoy, Jack, *Ulster's Joan of Arc, An Examination of the Betsy Gray Story*
(Bangor, 1989).

McKnight, Thomas, *Ulster As It Is* (London, 1896).

McNeill, Mary, *The Life and Times of Mary Ann McCracken,1770–1866*
(Dublin, 1960).

Maguire, W.A., *Up in Arms: the 1798 Rebellion in Ireland, Record of an
Exhibition at the Ulster Museum* (Belfast, 1998).

Ó Broin, Leon, *Revolutionary Underground: the Story of the Irish
Republican Brotherhood 1858–1924* (Dublin, 1976).

Pakenham, Thomas, *The Year of Liberty, the Story of the Great Irish
Rebellion of 1798* (London, 1969).

Reid, Archie R. (ed.), *The Liberty Tree* (Newtownabbey, 1998).

Robinson, Kenneth, *North Down and Ards in 1798* (Bangor, 1998).

Stewart, A.T.Q., *A Deeper Silence: the Hidden Origins of the United
Irishmen* (London, 1993).

Stewart, A.T.Q., *The Summer Soldiers: the 1798 Rebellion in Antrim and
Down* (Belfast, 1995).

Sullivan, A.M., *The Story of Ireland* (first published 1867).

Walker, B.M., *Past and Present: History, Identity and Politics in Ireland*
(Belfast, 2000).

Whelan, Kevin, *The Tree of Liberty: Radicalism, Catholicism and the
Construction of Irish Identity 1760–1830* (Cork, 1996).

Whelan, Kevin, *Fellowship of Freedom: the United Irishmen and 1798* (Cork, 1998).
Wilsdon, W., *The Sites of the 1798 Rising in Antrim and Down* (Belfast, 1997).

NEWSPAPERS

Belfast Evening Telegraph (later *Belfast Telegraph*)
Belfast Newsletter
Down Recorder
Longford Leader
Irish Independent
Irish Press
Irish Times
Newtownards Chronicle
Northern Whig
Sunday Times
United Irishman
Wexford Independent
Workers' Republic

JOURNALS AND PERIODICALS

Eighteenth Century Life, Vol. 2 (1999).
Éire–Ireland, Vols XXIII (1988), XXVIII (1992).
History Ireland, Vol. 6, no. 2, Summer 1998.
New Hibernia Review, Vol. II, Spring 1998, pp. 9–25.
Shan Van Vocht, 1897–9.

COMMEMORATIVE PAMPHLETS

Ballinamuck Bicentenary Committee, *1798–1998*.
Boolavogue Bicententennial Development Committee 1998, *Boolavogue 1798–1998*.
Dublin '98 Commemoration Committee, *Who Fears to Speak* (Dublin, 1948).
Belfast Commemoration Committee 1948, *Ninety-Eight*.
Comóradh '98, *Vinegar Hill Day, Enniscorthy, 21 June 1998*.

Notes

1 Kevin Whelan, *The Tree of Liberty: Radicalism, Catholicism and the Construction of Irish Identity 1760–1830* (Cork, 1996), p. 133. See the chapter "'98 after '98' for an excellent discussion of the disputed legacy of the United Irishmen in the nineteenth century.

2 For a perceptive and comprehensive account of the changing nature of Presbyterian attitudes to 1798 in the nineteenth century see Ian McBride, 'Memory and forgetting: Ulster Presbyterians and 1798', in *The 1798 Rebellion, a bicentenary perspective* T. Bartlett, D. Dickson, D. Keogh and K. Whelan (eds) (Dublin, forthcoming).

3 W.S. Dickson, *A Narrative of the Confinement and Exile of William Steel Dickson, D.D.* (Dublin, 1812).

4 Quoted in Finlay Holmes, *The Presbyterian Church in Ireland: a Popular History* (Dublin, 2000), p. 83.

5 The word 'Jacquerie' is frequently used by historians of 1798. It is borrowed from the French historians who used it originally to describe a peasant rising against the nobles in 1357–8.

6 Quoted in Dublin '98, the Dublin Commemoration Committee's 1948 pamphlet 'Who Fears to Speak' (see below).

7 Quoted in Whelan, op. cit., p. 150.

8 Ibid.

9 Ibid.

10 Ibid.

11 Ibid.

12 Ibid.

13 Ibid, p. 151.

14 Ibid.

15 Ibid.

16 In this present work the name 'Derry' has been used consistently for the city and county also known as 'Londonderry'.

17 After Arius of Alexandria who, during the period of the early Church, denied the full divinity of Christ.

18 This myth has been perpetuated and more recently has been given expression by Rev. Ian Paisley.

19 Quoted in Kevin Whelan, *Fellowship of Freedom: the United Irishmen and 1798* (Cork, 1998), p. 125.

20 It had initially been the preserve of members of the Established Church.

21 Kenneth Robinson, *North Down and Ards in 1798* (Bangor, 1998), p. 107.

22 Thomas McKnight, *Ulster As It Is* (London, 1896), Vol. 1, pp. 22–3.

23 See Holmes, op. cit.

24 Reprinted, with a new introduction by Ian Adamson, by Farset Publications (Belfast, 1998).

25 Whelan, *Tree of Liberty*, op. cit.

26 There are many extant versions. The version above is from an MS in Trinity College Dublin, reproduced in *Up in Arms: the 1798 Rebellion in Ireland*, Record of an Exhibition at the Ulster Museum (Belfast, 1998), p. 300.

27 *Irish News*, 16 Sept. 1948.

28 F.S.L. Lyons, *Ireland Since the Famine* (London, 1973).

29 Myles Byrne's Memoirs have been republished for the '98 bicentenary (Enniscorthy, 1998) with a new introduction by Thomas Bartlett.

30 Anna Kinsella, '1798 claimed for Catholics: Father Kavanagh, Fenians and the centenary celebrations', in Daire Keogh and Nicholas Furlong (eds), *The Mighty Wave: the 1798 Rebellion in Wexford* (Dublin, 1998), p. 146.

31 Gary Owens, 'Nationalist monuments in Ireland, c.1870–1914: symbolism and ritual', in Brian P. Kennedy and Raymond Gillespie (eds), *Ireland: Art into History* (Dublin, 1994), p. 105.

32 Quoted in Whelan, *Tree of Liberty*, op. cit., p. 169.

33 Article by Seamus Burke in *Boolavogue*

1798–1998, pp. 32–3, published by
Boolavogue Bicententennial
Development Committee.

34 Whelan, *Tree of Liberty*, op. cit., p. 169.

35 Fr Kavanagh, *Wexford People*, 15 June
1898, quoted in Whelan, op. cit.,
p. 171.

36 T.J. O'Keefe, in two articles in
'Éire–Ireland', provides the best
description of the centenary, particularly in dealing with the shenanigans
among the factions in Dublin. T.J.
O'Keefe, 'The 1898 efforts to celebrate
the United Irishmen: the '98
Centennial', 'Éire–Ireland', Vol. XXIII
(1988), and '"Who fears to speak of
'98?": the rhetoric and rituals of the
United Irishmen Centennial 1898',
'Éire–Ireland', Vol. XXVIII (1992).

37 *Shan Van Vocht*, 6 Sept. 1897.

38 *Irish News*, Sept. 1897; thanks for the
reference to this in her lecture 'The
Heroic Irish Women of 1798 and
1898' to Catherine Morris; see also
Sheila T. Johnston, *Alice: a Life of Alice
Milligan* (Omagh, 1994).

39 Ibid., Johnston and Morris.

40 Published as an historical facsimile by
the United Irish Commemoration
Society (Belfast, 1998).

41 See Johnston, op. cit.

42 A prominent '98 author.

43 *Irish News*, 7 June 1898.

44 *The Irish News*, in the days after the
march, devoted much copy to the rioters, contrasting their behaviour
unfavourably with that of the proces-
sionists. Even the *Belfast Newsletter*, a
strongly Unionist paper, conceded on
the day after that 'The city cannot clear
itself of the shame and humiliation that
have overtaken it'. *The Telegraph* of 8
June, while not condoning the riots,
made a point of contrasting the good
reception by Loyalists of the military
with the intense hostility shown to the
police.

45 Quoted in Finlay Holmes, 'From rebels
to Unionists', in Ronnie Hanna (ed.),
*The Union: Essays on Ireland and the
British Connection* (Newtownards,
2001), p. 44.

46 Quoted in Holmes, *Presbyterian Church
in Ireland*, p. 120.

47 Quoted in R.F. Holmes, 'United
Irishmen and Unionists: Irish
Presbyterians, 1791 and 1886', 'Studies
in Church History, Vol. 25: The
Churches, Ireland and the Irish'
(1989), p. 188.

48 Rev. Dr Richard Routledge Kane was
something of an enigma. A rather controversial figure, regarded as a hardliner,
he was involved in opposing Catholic
expansion in the city, notably the
building of the Mater Hospital by the
Irish Sisters of Mercy. However, he was
at the same time a member of the
Gaelic League in Belfast and often
signed Lodge minutes in the Irish version of his name.

49 *Belfast Evening Telegraph*, 2 June 1898.

50 Ibid., 7 June 1898.

51 Ibid., 6 June 1898.

52 *Down Recorder*, 16 July 1898, quoted
in Jack McCoy, *Ulster's Joan of Arc, An
Examination of the Betsy Gray Story*
(Bangor, 1989), pp. 33–4.

53 *Irish News*, 11 Aug. 1898.

54 Ibid., 15 Aug. 1898.

55 See O'Keefe, 'Rhetoric and rituals', op.
cit., p. 75.

56 Naturally the Catholic religious context
of this date was also pointed out in the
Belfast Newsletter, Northern Whig and
Irish Times, 16 Aug. 1898.

57 A very good description of the events
of 'Wolfe Tone Day' is given in Owens,
op. cit., pp. 103–117.

58 *Irish News*, 16 Aug. 1898.

59 *Belfast Evening Telegraph*, 16 Aug.
1898.

60 Leon Ó Broin, *Revolutionary
Underground: the Story of the Irish
Republican Brotherhood 1858–1924*
(Dublin, 1976), p. 91.

61 The Wolfe Tone memorial foundation
stone, after years of languishing in stor-
age, was ceremonially installed in a site
adjoining the newly opened 'Croppies'

Acre' Garden of Remembrance, in front of Collins Barracks, Dublin, at the end of the bicentenary in 1998.

62 *Wexford Independent*, 2 Nov. 1898.

63 For a review of '98 monuments, Owens (op. cit.) is worth looking at. See also *Epitaph of 1798: a Photographic Record of 1798 Memorials in the Island of Ireland and Beyond* (Enniscorthy, 2002).

64 Maud Gonne, *A Servant of the Queen* (Dublin, 1938), pp. 271–2.

65 For a comprehensive account of this subject see Lawrence W. McBride, 'Historical imagery in Irish political illustrations, 1880–1910', in *New Hibernia Review*, Vol. II, Spring 1998, pp. 9–25.

66 A.M. Sullivan, *The Story of Ireland* (first published 1867).

67 Inspector General's Monthly Confidential Reports (PRO LONDON, CO 904/68), quoted in Virginia Crossman, 'The Shan Van Vocht: women, republicanism and the commemoration of the 1798 Rebellion', 'Eighteenth Century Life, Vol. 2' (1999). I am grateful to Virginia Crossman for sending me this material.

68 Ibid.

69 PRO LONDON, CO 904/70; see Crossman, op. cit.

70 First published in Arthur Griffith's *United Irishman*, 24 Feb. 1900.

71 *Longford Leader*, 15 Sept. 1928. See also Ballinamuck Bicentenary 1798–1998.

72 A somewhat unidiomatic 'God free Ireland'.

73 *Longford Leader*, 15 Sept. 1928.

74 *Irish Independent*, 27 June 1938.

75 Following in his father Sir Thomas Esmonde's footsteps.

76 *Irish Independent*, 21 June 1948.

77 See *Irish Independent* and *Irish Press* June–Nov. 1948.

78 *Irish Independent*, 12 July 1948.

79 Ibid.

80 Ibid., 19 July 1948.

81 Ibid., 26 July 1948.

82 Ibid, 2 Aug. 1948. The banner headline proclaimed 'Taoiseach Renews Irish Unity Plea – Vital Reasons For Ending Of Partition'.

83 Ibid., 2 Aug. 1948.

84 Sam McAllister, a Protestant United Irishman from Co. Antrim, had joined Michael Dwyer in his rearguard struggle in 1799 and had helped him to escape capture at the cottage at Derrynamuck.

85 *Irish Independent*, 23 Aug. 1948.

86 Ibid.

87 James Craig (1st Viscount Craigavon) was Prime Minister of Northern Ireland from 1921 to his death in 1940.

88 *Irish Independent*, 15 Nov. 1948.

89 Ibid., 16 Nov. 1948.

90 Ibid.

91 Ibid., 22 Nov. 1948.

92 Ibid.

93 *Irish News*, 14 Sept. 1948.

94 James Stewart is a member of the UICS and has kindly given permission to include here extracts from his as yet unpublished account of his part in the 1948 commemorations at the Bone area and in the march to Cave Hill.

95 *Irish News*, 13 Sept. 1948.

96 Ibid., 18 Sept. 1948.

97 Ibid., 23 Sept. 1948.

98 Interviewed in *Belfast Telegraph*, 3 Apr. 1997.

99 My thanks to Bernard Browne, Comóradh '98, for providing copy.

100 *Irish Independent*, 20 Nov. 1967.

101 Bigger's association with the centenary is the probable reason.

102 David Dickson, Daire Keogh and Kevin Whelan (eds), *The United Irishmen: Radicalism, Republicanism and Rebellion* (Dublin, 1993).

103 *Newtownards Chronicle*, 19 Feb. 1998.

104 Ibid.

105 *The Liberty Tree: the story of the United Irishmen in and around the borough of Newtownabbey*.

106 *Sunday Times*, 2 Mar. 1997.

107 *Irish Times*, Saturday, 13 June 1998.

108 *Irish Times*, 25 Nov. 1998.

109 T. Bartlett, D. Dickson, D. Keogh, K. Whelan (eds), *The 1798 Rebellion, a bicentenary perspective* (Dublin, 2003).

110 For the history of 1798 in Boolavogue and subsequent commemorations, see the excellent *Boolavogue 1798–1998*, produced to mark the opening of the Fr Murphy Centre at Tomnaboley, officially opened by President McAleese on 30 May 1998.

111 On that day the first sod was cut by US Ambassador Jean Kennedy Smith for a modern memorial Tulach a' tSolais, erected at the battle site. See Brian Cleary, *The Battle of Oulart Hill, 1798: Context and Strategy* (Naas, 1999) for an account of the battle and 1798 in the locality.

112 *Irish Times*, 9 Sept. 1998.

113 Mary McNeill, *The Life and Times of Mary Ann McCracken, 1770–1866* (Dublin, 1960).

114 Thomas Pakenham, *The Year of Liberty, the Story of the Great Irish Rebellion of 1798* (London, 1969).

115 L.M. Cullen, *The Emergence of Modern Ireland 1600–1900* (London, 1981); 'The 1798 Rebellion in its eighteenth-century context', in Patrick J. Corish (ed.), Radicals, Rebels and Establishments (Belfast, 1985).

116 Marianne Elliott, *Partners in Revolution: the United Irishmen and France* (New Haven, 1982) and *Wolfe Tone: Prophet of Irish Independence* (New Haven, 1989).

117 Including A.T.Q. Stewart, *A Deeper Silence: the Hidden Origins of the United Irishmen* (London, 1993) and *The Summer Soldiers: the 1798 Rebellion in Antrim and Down* (Belfast, 1995).

118 Thomas Bartlett, *The Fall and Rise of the Irish Nation: the Catholic Question 1690–1830* (Dublin, 1992) and Tom Bartlett (ed.), *Life of Theobald Wolfe Tone*, Compiled and Arranged by William Theobald Wolfe Tone (Dublin, 1998).

119 N.J. Curtin, *The United Irishmen: Popular Politics in Ulster and Dublin* (Oxford, 1994).

120 See particularly Whelan, *The Tree of Liberty*, op. cit.

121 Daire Keogh and Nicholas Furlong (eds), *The Women of 1798* (Dublin, 1998).

122 Daire Keogh and Nicholas Furlong (eds), *The Mighty Wave: the 1798 Rebellion in Wexford* (Dublin, 1998), Myrtle Hill, Brian Turner and Kenneth Dawson (eds), *The 1798 Rebellion in Down* (Newtownards, 1998).

123 Allan Blackstock, *An Ascendancy Army: the Yeomanry 1796–1834* (Dublin, 1998).

124 *History Ireland*, Vol. 6, no. 2, Summer 1998.

125 R.F. Foster, *The Irish Story: Telling Tales and Making It Up In Ireland* (London, 2001).

126 Thomas Bartlett, 'Sticking to the past', review in *Times Literary Supplement*, 25 Jan. 2002.

127 Foster, op. cit., pp. 227–8.

128 Ibid., p. 228.

129 Ibid., p. 229.

130 Ibid.

131 Ibid., p. 226.

132 Bartlett, 'Sticking to the past', op. cit., p. 28.

133 Ibid.

134 Rev. Kennaway and other members of the Education Committee resigned in the summer of 2000.

135 *Irish News*, 1 Oct. 1999.

Index